MW00931071

LEARN SPANISH WITH SHORT STORIES FOR ADULT BEGINNERS

Shortcut Your Spanish Fluency!
(Fun & Easy Reads)

© Copyright 2022 - All rights reserved.

The content contained within this book may not be reproduced, duplicated or transmitted without direct written permission from the author or the publisher.

Under no circumstances will any blame or legal responsibility be held against the publisher, or author, for any damages, reparation, or monetary loss due to the information contained within this book, either directly or indirectly.

Legal Notice:

This book is copyright protected. It is only for personal use. You cannot amend, distribute, sell, use, quote or paraphrase any part, or the content within this book, without the consent of the author or publisher.

Disclaimer Notice:

Please note the information contained within this document is for educational and entertainment purposes only. All effort has been executed to present accurate, up to date, reliable, complete information. No warranties of any kind are declared or implied. Readers acknowledge that the author is not engaging in the rendering of legal, financial, medical or professional advice. The content within this book has been derived from various sources. Please consult a licensed professional before attempting any techniques outlined in this book.

By reading this document, the reader agrees that under no circumstances is the author responsible for any losses, direct or indirect, that are incurred as a result of the use of information contained within this document, including, but not limited to, errors, omissions, or inaccuracies.

Table of Contents

~~$29~~ FREE BONUSES

Complete Spanish Phrasebook
+ Digital Spanish Flashcards Download

Scan QR code above to claim your free bonuses

OR

visit exploretowin.com/vipbonus

Ready To Start Speaking Spanish?

**Inside this Complete Spanish Phrasebook
+ digital Spanish flashcards combo you'll:**

✓ **Say what you want:** learn the most common words and phrases used in Spanish, so you can express yourself clearly, the first time!

✓ **Avoid awkward fumbling:** explore core Spanish grammar principles to avoid situations where you're left blank, not knowing what to say.

✓ **Improved recall:** Confidently express yourself in Spanish by learning high-frequency verbs & conjugations - taught through fun flashcards!

Scan QR code above to claim your free bonuses

OR

visit exploretowin.com/vipbonus

Introduction

You know Spanish is one of the most spoken languages in the world, right? That it is one of the official languages of over 20 countries, which means that being able to speak it can open a door or two for you? And we're not only talking about professional opportunities here, but also the chance of communicating with its many speakers and experiencing a variety of rich cultures.

So, if you've recently added learning Spanish to your bucket list, then buying this book was the right call. After countless hours online, you're probably tired of finding nothing but stories for children, or worse: no reading material at all. *Learn Spanish with Short stories for Adult Beginners* delivers high-quality short stories with exercises specifically designed for you, our very much adult reader. Learning a new language is daunting enough on its own. Let's not make it more complicated than it has to be.

Our short stories are carefully tailored to beginner learners, with vocabulary and structures that get progressively harder as you go on. However, we won't cover concepts that might be too hard for you, and all vocabulary that may seem complicated will be explained in the glossary at the end of each story. Through this method, you will feel a sense of achievement as you notice your Spanish language skills constantly improving.

So, whether you're a true beginner who can barely say "hola", or a more trained learner who's looking for new entertaining material to read, *Learn Spanish with Short stories for Adult Beginners* is the right book for you.

How to use this book

You will notice each story in our book follows the same structure:

Short story in Spanish

A summary in Spanish

A summary in English

A glossary with Spanish words and phrases and their English translation

Quizzes to test your understanding of the story

Answers to check your work

We suggest you follow these tips to get the most out of our stories:

1) **Read the story all the way through**. Don't worry about trying to understand every single word right away. Follow the plot of the story as much as you can, and use the context to fill in those mental gaps you may have.

2) **Take a moment to reflect on the plot of the story**. Think about how much you were able to understand on your own. If it helps, write down in English what you think the story was about.

3) **Read the Spanish summary**. See if the idea of the story is the same you had in your head. If the Spanish

summary seems too complicated at first, try reading the English one. And don't worry, even if it feels hard at first, it will get easier as you train your mind.

4) **Read the story once again**. This time, try focusing on the details you may have missed on your first read.

5) **Review the glossary**. Make sure you understand the words in the list. If you're unsure of the meaning of any of the words, go back to the story to put them in context. This will help you fully grasp the meaning of the more complicated phrases or expressions.

6) **Test yourself**. Answer the quizzes to make sure you understood the story from beginning to end.

7) **Check your answers**. Make sure your answers are similar or the same as the ones at the end of the chapter. Don't worry if you don't get all the answers right, though. Making mistakes isn't failing. If you made a mistake, review that part of the story. You'll have a better understanding of both the story as a whole and the concept, phrase or structure that you didn't get the first time around.

8) **Congratulate yourself**. Think about how much you understood on your own, even if it wasn't much at first. Remember that the key to learning a new language is to practice. The more you read and train your brain, the better you will get at this.

9) **Go to the next story**. Once you've gotten everything you could out of the story, go to the next one! Remember that each story has its own set of structures and vocabulary that gets progressively more challenging. The more you read, the closer you will be to your goal of mastering the Spanish language.

Chapter 1:
El nuevo trabajo – The new job

El trabajo más productivo es el que sale de las manos de un hombre contento.
\- Victor Pauchet

Hoy es el **primer día** de Luis en su nuevo trabajo en la empresa Future Technologies. Luis **llega a** la oficina **a tiempo**. **Está muy nervioso** pero sus **compañeros de trabajo lo reciben con los brazos abiertos**.

–**Mucho gusto**, ¿cómo te **llamas?**

–Mucho gusto, **me llamo** Luis.

–**Bienvenido**, Luis.

Carolina, **la jefa de Luis**, lo acompaña **en todo momento**. Le da un tour del edificio, pasan por la cafetería, la recepción, **el área de descanso**. Ahí **conoce** a otros **desarrolladores web como él** y **se presenta nuevamente**.

—Mucho gusto, Luis —dice un hombre alto.

—**¿Cuáles son sus nombres**?

—**Mi nombre es** Carlos y **ella se llama** Lucía.

—**Un placer** —dice Luis. **Al otro lado de la mesa** Luis ve a más personas conversando. —**¿Quiénes son ellos**?

—Ellos son Javier, Mario y Ana. Son muy **amables y conversadores** —dice Lucía.

—¿Cuál es tu **apellido**, Luis? —pregunta Carlos.

—Alvarado.

—**¿Cómo se deletrea** Alvarado?

—A - L - V - A - R - A - D - O.

—**¿Y de dónde eres**?

—**Soy de** Medellín. ¿Ustedes de dónde son?

—Nosotros somos de acá, de Bogotá —responde Lucía.

Luego de tomar una taza de café con Carlos y Lucía, Luis va a su **lugar de trabajo**. La oficina es **grande, luminosa, y hay varios escritorios** de madera. Lucía trabaja en **la misma** oficina que Luis. Su escritorio **está adornado con** algunas plantas y **retratos** de su familia. Lucía **le cuenta a Luis que su hijo tiene siete años** y **va en segundo grado de primaria**.

—**¿A qué se dedica tu esposo**? —pregunta Luis.

—**Mi esposo es ingeniero** y **trabaja en** esta misma compañía. ¿Tienes hijos?

—Sí, **tengo un niño y una niña**.

—**¿Cuántos años tienen tus hijos**?

—Mi hijo tiene tres años y **mi hija tiene dos**.

El resto de la mañana es **bastante tranquila**. Luis **almuerza** con sus compañeros y **se adapta a la perfección** a su nuevo trabajo. **Al final del día**, Luis **se despide** de Lucía y **se va** a casa.

Resumen

Un hombre llamado Luis empieza su primer día en un nuevo trabajo en una empresa llamada Future Technologies. Su jefa, Carolina, le muestra el edificio y terminan en el área de descanso, donde conoce a dos desarrolladores web, Lucía y Carlos. Conversa un rato con sus nuevos compañeros de trabajo y luego se va a su lugar de trabajo. Ahí comparte un poco más de su vida con Lucía. Se adapta muy bien a su nuevo trabajo y al final del día, se va a casa.

Summary

A man named Luis starts his first day at a new job at a company called Future Technologies. His boss, Carolina, shows him around the building and they end up in the break room, where he meets two web developers, Lucía and Carlos. He makes small talk with his new coworkers and then he goes to his workspace. There, he shares a bit more about his life with Lucía. He adapts really well to his new job, and at the end of the day, he goes home.

Glosario – Glossary

Primer día: first day

Llega a: he arrives to

A tiempo: on time

Está muy nervioso: he is very nervous

Compañeros de trabajo: coworkers

Lo reciben con los brazos abiertos: they welcome him with open arms

Mucho gusto: nice to meet you

¿Cómo te llamas?: what's your name?

(Yo) me llamo: my name is

Bienvenido: welcome

La jefa de Luis: Luis's boss

En todo momento: at all times

El área de descanso: the break room

Conoce: he meets

Desarrolladores web: web developers

Como él: like him

Se presenta: he introduces himself

Nuevamente: again

¿Cuáles son sus nombres?: what are your names?

Mi nombre es: my name is

Ella se llama: her name is

¿Quiénes son ellos?: who are they?

Amables y conversadores: kind and talkative

Apellido: last name

¿Cómo se deletrea...?: how do you spell...?

¿De dónde eres?: where are you from?

(Yo) soy de: I am from

Lugar de trabajo: workspace

Grande y luminosa: big and well-lit

Hay varios escritorios: there are several desks

La misma: the same

Está adornado con: it is decorated with

Retratos: pictures

Le cuenta a Luis que: she tells Luis that

Su hijo tiene siete años: her son is seven years old

Va en segundo grado de primaria: he is in the second grade of elementary school

¿A qué se dedica tu esposo?: what does your husband do?

Mi esposo es ingeniero: my husband is an engineer

Trabaja en: he works at

¿Tienes hijos?: do you have any children?

Tengo un niño y una niña: I have a boy and a girl

¿Cuántos años tienen tus hijos?: how old are your children?

Mi hija tiene dos: my daughter is two

Bastante tranquila: pretty calm

Almuerza: he has lunch

Se adapta a la perfección: he adapts perfectly

Al final del día: at the end of the day

Se despide de: he says goodbye to

Se va: he leaves

Ejercicio 1

Contesta las siguientes preguntas – answer the following questions

1- **¿Cómo se siente Luis?** – how's Luis feeling?

_____

2- **¿Cómo se llama la jefa de Luis?** – what's Luis's boss name?

_____

3- **¿A qué se dedica Luis?** – what does Luis do?

_____

4- **¿Cómo son Javier, Mario y Ana?** – what are Javier, Mario and Ana like?

_____

5- **¿Cuál es el apellido de Luis?** – what's Luis's last name?

_____

6- **¿De dónde son Carlos y Lucía?** – where are Carlos and Lucía from?

_____

7- **¿Cómo es la oficina de Luis?** – what is Luis's office like?

_____

8- **¿Cuántos años tiene el hijo de Lucía?** – how old is Lucía's son?

_____

9- ¿Dónde trabaja el esposo de Lucía? – where does Lucía's husband work at?

_____

10- ¿Cuántos hijos tiene Luis? – how many children does Luis have?

_____

Ejercicio 2

Elige entre "verdadero" o "falso" – choose "true" or "false"

1- **Luis llega tarde a su primer día de trabajo.** – Luis arrives late to his first day at work.

_____

2- **Carolina es amiga de Luis.** – Carolina is Luis's friend.

_____

3- **Luis conoce a Lucía en la cafetería.** – Luis meets Lucía in the cafeteria.

_____

4- **Luis es de Medellín.** – Luis is from Medellín.

_____

5- **Carlos es de Barranquilla.** – Carlos is from Barranquilla.

_____

6- **El escritorio de Luis es de madera.** – Luis' desk is made of wood.

_____

7- **Lucía solo tiene libros en su escritorio.** – Lucía only has books on her desk.

_____

8- **El hijo de Lucía va en segundo grado.** – Lucía's son is in second grade.

_____

9- **Luis tiene tres hijos.** – Luis has three children.

10- **El esposo de Lucía es ingeniero.** – Lucía's husband is an engineer.

Respuestas – Answers

Ejercicio 1

1- Luis está nervioso.

2- La jefa de Luis se llama Carolina.

3- Luis es desarrollador web.

4- Javier, Mario y Ana son amables y conversadores.

5- El apellido de Luis es Alvarado.

6- Carlos y Lucía son de Bogotá.

7- La oficina de Luis es grande y luminosa.

8- El hijo de Lucía tiene siete años.

9- El esposo de Lucía trabaja en la misma empresa que ella.

10- Luis tiene dos hijos.

Ejercicio 2

1- Falso

2- Falso

3- Falso

4- Verdadero

5- Falso

6- Verdadero

7- Falso

8- Verdadero

9- Falso

10- Verdadero

Puntos clave – Key takeaways

- To say our name in Spanish, we use the verb *llamar* reflexively with the reflexive pronoun *se*.
- The reflexive pronoun *se* has five different conjugations (*me, te, se, nos, se*).
- One of the uses of the verb *ser* is to talk about where we're from.
- The verb *ser* has five different conjugations (*soy, eres, es, somos, son*).
- One of the uses of the verb tener is to talk about our age.
- The verb tener has five different conjugations (*tengo, tienes, tiene, tenemos, tienen*).
- To talk about our job, we use the verb *dedicar* reflexively with the reflexive pronoun *se*.

In the next chapter, you will learn how to use the verb *estar*, how to tell time, and some parts of the house.

Chapter 2:
¿Dónde está Carlos? – Where's Carlos?

Una madre, nunca está sola en sus pensamientos. Una madre siempre piensa dos veces, una en sí misma y otra en su niño.
- Sophia Loren

Marisol llega a casa luego de **un largo día en el trabajo.** Va a **la cocina** y **saluda** a su hija Anabel. **Le pregunta por su hermano** Carlos.

–**Quizás está en el jardín** –dice Anabel.

Marisol **se acerca al jardín** pero **Carlos no está ahí**.

–**Tal vez** está en su **cuarto** – dice Anabel.

Marisol va al cuarto de Carlos pero **no hay nadie**. Marisol **revisa el baño, la sala, el comedor, incluso va al balcón,** donde están las plantas. **No sabe dónde está su hijo** Carlos y **está muy preocupada**.

–Anabel, ¿**dónde está tu hermano**?

–**No sé**, mamá.

–**¿Qué hora es?**

Anabel dice que **son las 7 p.m. Marisol piensa que Carlos está con su mejor amigo**, José, **así que llama a casa de José. El padre de José contesta el teléfono**.

–**Aló**, **buenas tardes**.

–Buenas tardes, soy Marisol, **la mamá de Carlos**. **¿De casualidad** mi hijo está en su casa **jugando con José**?

–Hola, Marisol. No, Carlos no está aquí.

–Estoy muy preocupada. Carlos **sale de la escuela a las 3 de la tarde. A esta hora** él siempre está en la casa.

–**¿Tienes el número de sus otros amigos**?

–Carlos tiene **pocos** amigos. Su mejor amigo es José.

–Le voy a preguntar a José por Carlos. **Dame un minuto.**

Marisol **espera junto al teléfono**. Piensa en **el horario** de su hijo. **Los martes** Carlos tiene **clases de matemáticas de 8 de la mañana a 10 de la mañana.** De 10 a.m. al **mediodía** tiene **clases de educación física**. Del mediodía a 1 p.m. es su **hora de almuerzo**. Por último, de 1 p.m. a 3 p.m. tiene su **clase de arte**. Carlos siempre llega a casa **antes de las 4 p.m.**

–Marisol, **anota** el número de otro amigo de Carlos –dice el papá de José. –Tal vez Carlos está con él.

Marisol anota el número en un papel y llama **inmediatamente**.

–Aló, ¿David?

–Buenas tardes, no. Soy Marisol, la madre de Carlos, un amigo de David.

–¿Mi hijo está con **usted**?

–No, **de hecho** llamo **para preguntar si** mi hijo Carlos está en su casa.

–No, Marisol, no sabemos dónde está nuestro hijo **tampoco**.

–**¿Y si están juntos? ¿Sabe dónde pueden estar?**

–No sé, pero **voy a salir a buscarlos** en **el parque** cerca de la casa.

–Es una buena idea. Voy a ir con usted.

Marisol va a **la parada de autobús. Son las 7 y media.** Toma el autobús 35 que **la deja a una cuadra** del Parque Simón Bolívar. Ahí **se encuentra con la mamá de David**, el amiguito de Carlos. **En su rostro** ve que **la mujer está tan estresada y preocupada como ella.** Marisol ve la hora en su reloj, **son las 8 en punto.**

–Mira, Marisol –dice la mamá de David.

El parque es inmenso. **Algunas mujeres hacen yoga** y **otros pasean a sus perros.** David y Carlos **corren detrás de un perrito** y **sonríen.** Marisol y la mamá de David **se apresuran y abrazan** a sus hijos. Los niños **están sorprendidos**, y luego **arrepentidos.** Dicen que **olvidaron la hora** y como es verano **aún está soleado.** Marisol se despide de David y su mamá. Junto a su hijo **toma un autobús de vuelta a casa. Marisol está feliz de tener a su hijo en sus brazos,** pero cuando llegan a casa **le dice que está castigado. Está muy molesta. Aliviada,** pero molesta. Carlos **la entiende** y **le pide disculpas. Marisol le da un beso en la mejilla** y un largo abrazo. Mira el reloj. **Falta un cuarto para las 9, ya es hora de cenar.** Cuando **son 20 pasadas las 10**, Carlos **se cepilla los dientes** y **va a la cama porque está cansado. Marisol le lee una historia para dormir** y **le desea dulces sueños.**

Resumen

Una mujer llamada Marisol vuelve a casa luego de un largo día de trabajo y se da cuenta de que su hijo, Carlos, no está en la casa. Ella se preocupa y llama a los amigos de su hijo para saber dónde está. La madre de otro niño le dice que su hijo tampoco ha llegado a casa y juntas van al parque a buscar a sus hijos. Por suerte, los niños están en el parque jugando. Marisol vuelve a casa con su hijo y lo castiga por lo que hizo. Al final, ella le lee una historia para dormir a Carlos y le desea dulces sueños.

Summary

A woman named Marisol comes back home after a long day of work and realizes that her son, Carlos, is not home. She gets worried and calls her son's friends to find out where he is. Another boy's mom tells her that her son is not home either and they both go to the park to go look for their sons. Luckily, the kids are at the park playing around. Marisol goes back home with her son and grounds him for what he did. At the end, she reads Carlos a bedtime story and wishes him sweet dreams.

Glosario – Glossary

Un largo día en el trabajo: a long day of work

La cocina: the kitchen

Le pregunta por su hermano: she asks her for her brother

Quizás está en el jardín: maybe he is in the garden

Se acerca al jardín: she approaches the garden

Carlos no está ahí: Carlos is not there

Tal vez: maybe

Cuarto: bedroom

No hay nadie: there is no one (there)

Revisa el baño: she checks the bathroom

La sala: the living room

El comedor: the dining room

Incluso va al balcón: she even goes to the balcony

No sabe dónde está su hijo: she doesn't know where her son is

Está muy preocupada: she is very worried

¿Dónde está tu hermano?: where is your brother?

(Yo) no sé: I don't know

¿Qué hora es?: what time is it?

Son las 7 p.m.: it is 7 p.m.

Marisol piensa que Carlos está con su mejor amigo: Marisol thinks that Carlos is with his best friend

Así que llama a casa de José: so she calls Jose's house

El padre de José contesta el teléfono: José's dad picks up the phone

Aló, buenas tardes: hi, good afternoon

La mamá de Carlos: Carlos's mom

De casualidad: by any chance

Jugando con José: playing with José

Sale de la escuela a las 3 de la tarde: he leaves school at 3 in the afternoon

A esta hora: at this time

¿Tienes el número de sus otros amigos?: do you have the number of his other friends?

Pocos: few

Dame un minuto: give me a minute

Espera junto al teléfono: she waits by the phone

El horario: the schedule

Los martes: on Tuesdays

Clases de matemáticas: math classes

De 8 de la mañana a 10 de la mañana: from 8 in the morning to 10 in the morning

Mediodía: noon

Clases de educación física: physical education classes

Hora de almuerzo: lunch break

Clase de arte: art class

Antes de las 4 p.m.: before 4 p.m.

Anota: write down

Inmediatamente: immediately

Usted: you (formal)

De hecho: in fact

Para preguntar: to ask

Tampoco: neither

¿Y si están juntos?: what if they are together?

¿Sabe dónde pueden estar?: do you know where they might be?

Voy a salir a buscarlos: I'm going to go out to look for them

El parque: the park

La parada de autobús: the bus stop

Son las 7 y media: it is half past 7

La deja a una cuadra de...: it leaves her a block from...

Se encuentra con la mamá de David: she meets David's mom

En su rostro: in her face

La mujer está tan estresada y preocupada como ella: the woman is as stressed and worried as her

Son las 8 en punto: it is 8 o'clock

Algunas mujeres hacen yoga: some women do yoga

Otros pasean a sus perros: others walk their dogs

Corren detrás de un perrito: they run after a little dog

Sonríen: they smile

Se apresuran: they hurry up

Abrazan: they hug

Están sorprendidos: they are surprised

Arrepentidos: remorseful

Olvidaron la hora: they lost track of time

Aún está soleado: it is still sunny

Toma un autobús de vuelta a casa: she takes a bus back home

Marisol está feliz: Marisol is happy

De tener a su hijo en sus brazos: about having her son in her arms

Le dice que está castigado: she tells him he is grounded

Está muy molesta: she is very upset

Aliviada: relieved

La entiende: he understands her

Le pide disculpas: he apologizes

Marisol le da un beso en la mejilla: Marisol gives him a kiss on his cheek

Falta un cuarto para las 9: it is a quarter to 9

Es hora de cenar: it is time for dinner

Son 20 pasadas las 10: it is 20 past 10

Se cepilla los dientes: he brushes his teeth

Va a la cama porque está cansado: he goes to bed because he is tired

Marisol le lee una historia para dormir: Marisol reads him a bedtime story

Le desea dulces sueños: she wishes him sweet dreams

Ejercicio 1

Contesta las siguientes preguntas – answer the following questions

1- **¿Dónde está Anabel?** – where's Anabel?

_____

2- **¿Cómo se siente Marisol al no encontrar a su hijo?** – how does Marisol feel upon not finding her son?

_____

3- **¿A quién llama Marisol primero?** – who does Marisol call first?

_____

4- **¿Quién contesta el teléfono?** – who answers the phone?

_____

5- **¿A qué hora Carlos tiene clases de matemáticas?** – what time does Carlos have math class?

_____

6- **¿A quién llama Marisol después?** – who does Marisol call afterwards?

_____

7- **¿A dónde va Marisol a buscar a su hijo?** – where does Marisol go look for her son?

_____

8- **¿Qué hace Carlos cuando Marisol lo encuentra?** – what is Carlos doing when Marisol finds him?

_____

9- **¿Cuáles son las consecuencias por lo que Carlos hizo?** – what are the consequences for what Carlos did?

_____

10- **¿Qué hace Carlos antes de ir a la cama?** – what does Carlos do before going to bed?

_____

Ejercicio 2

Elige entre "verdadero" o "falso" – choose "true" or "false"

1- **Marisol estuvo en la casa todo el día.** – Marisol was home all day.

_____

2- **Carlos está en casa de José.** – Carlos is at José's place.

_____

3- **Carlos tiene clases de matemáticas los martes en la tarde.** – Carlos has math class on Tuesday afternoon.

_____

4- **Carlos siempre llega a casa antes de las 4 p.m.** – Carlos always gets home before 4 p.m.

_____

5- **Marisol toma el autobús 35.** – Marisol takes the bus 35.

_____

6- **A Marisol le toma una hora llegar al parque.** – It takes Marisol one hour to get to the park.

_____

7- **Carlos lee un libro en el parque.** – Carlos is reading a book at the park.

_____

8- **Marisol toma un taxi a casa.** – Marisol takes a taxi home.

_____

9- **Marisol llega a casa a un cuarto para las 9.** – Marisol gets home at a quarter to 9.

___

10- **Carlos va a la cama antes de las 10 p.m.** – Carlos goes to bed before 10 p.m.

___

Respuestas – Answers

Ejercicio 1

1- Anabel está en la cocina.

2- Marisol está muy preocupada.

3- Marisol llama a José, el amigo de Carlos.

4- El padre de José contesta el teléfono.

5- Carlos tiene clases de matemáticas de 10 a.m. al mediodía.

6- Marisol llama a David, otro amigo de Carlos.

7- Marisol va al parque a buscar a Carlos.

8- Carlos corre detrás de un perrito.

9- Marisol castiga a Carlos por lo que hizo.

10- Carlos se cepilla los dientes antes de ir a la cama.

Ejercicio 2

1- Falso

2- Falso

3- Falso

4- Verdadero

5- Verdadero

6- Falso

7- Falso

8- Falso

9- Verdadero

10- Falso

Puntos clave – Key takeaways

- One of the uses of the verb *estar* is to talk about where someone or something is.
- The verb *ser* has five different conjugations (*estoy, estás, está, estamos, están*).
- *Aló* is the Spanish phrase we use to answer the phone.
- When the time is 1 a.m. or 1 p.m., we say "es la una". With any other time, we say "son las..."

In the next chapter, you will learn vocabulary about relatives, some professions, and adjectives to describe certain feelings.

Chapter 3:
El regalo – The present

Los regalos se hacen para el placer de quien los da,
no para el mérito de quien los recibe.
- Carlos Ruiz Zafón

Hoy es **la boda** de Rosa, **la prima de Cristina**. Después de **la ceremonia en la iglesia** La Paz de Cristo, todos **los invitados** van a **una quinta alquilada** muy hermosa. **Además de** muchos amigos de **los novios, la familia** de Rosa está presente. Cristina ve a su **abuela** luego de cinco años. **Su abuelo no pudo asistir** porque **está enfermo**. Cristina **conversa** un poco con sus primos pero **está distraída, hablando** con su **novio** por teléfono. El novio de Cristina es  **el encargado de encontrar el regalo** perfecto para Rosa. Cristina sabe que es mucha **responsabilidad** para su novio, pero

él insistió. Ahora ella cree que **fue** un error. **Las tiendas** cierran a las 6 de la tarde los **sábados**. Encontrar un regalo puede ser difícil.

La tía de Cristina le da ideas para regalos. Le dice que algún **electrodoméstico sería** un buen regalo para una pareja de recién casados. **Le enseña** fotos de **licuadoras, microondas, batidoras** y **un juego de ollas**. **El esposo** de su amiga le sugiere comprar **un tostador**. **La madrina** de Cristina llega un poco tarde a la fiesta, pero tiene varios regalos en sus manos. Ella es **periodista** y **viaja** constantemente. Siempre que vuelve le regala un perfume nuevo a Cristina. **El primo** de Cristina, **un abogado** con **más deudas que dinero**, trae un regalo modesto. Cristina intenta **distraerse**. **Se toma fotos con su sobrina** y juega un rato con su **sobrino**. También **charla con su tío**, un **profesor de filosofía** que es muy **parlanchín**. Hablan sobre **la vida y el amor** por un largo rato.

Cristina llama a su novio.

—¿Dónde estás?

—Estoy en **el centro comercial** —responde su novio.

—**Por favor, apresúrate**.

Cristina **prueba unos postres de chocolate** exquisitos y **le pregunta al mesero cómo se llaman**. Su novio **no contesta los mensajes** y Cristina está estresada. **Se siente culpable** porque no **compró** el regalo de su prima con más tiempo. Ella siempre **deja todo para último minuto**.

El nuevo esposo de su prima conversa con ella un momento. **Es doctor** y le cuenta que la semana siguiente tiene varias **cirugías**. Por ahora **está de vacaciones** y está disfrutando de la fiesta. Rosa le pregunta a Cristina **si todo está bien**. Le dice que **parece** algo preocupada. Le muestra **unos zarcillos costosos que le regaló su padrino**, y Cristina **se siente**

peor. Piensa que **lo mejor es irse** de la fiesta **antes de pasar un momento vergonzoso**. Pero cuando **se preparan para cortar el pastel**, llega el novio de Cristina. **Está muy apenado por tardarse tanto**, pero cree que **encontró el regalo ideal** para la novia: **un reloj de oro** muy hermoso. Cristina **al fin está relajada** y **puede divertirse, bailar, comer y tomar**. Toma muchas fotos. **Quiere recordar el día con mucho cariño**.

Resumen

Cristina asiste a la boda de su prima, Rosa. Ahí se encuentra con varios miembros de su familia que tenía tiempo sin ver. Intenta disfrutar de la fiesta, pero está estresada porque aún no ha encontrado el regalo de bodas para su prima. Su novio está buscando el regalo perfecto justo en ese momento. Cristina habla con los invitados, se toma fotos y prueba distintos postres. Justo cuando Cristina piensa en irse de la fiesta, afortunadamente, su novio llega a tiempo con el regalo y ya los dos pueden disfrutar del resto de la noche con tranquilidad.

Summary

Cristina attends her cousin's wedding. There, she sees some of her relatives that she hadn't seen in a while. She tries to enjoy the party, but she's stressed because she still hasn't found her cousin's wedding gift. Her boyfriend is looking for her wedding gift at that very moment. Cristina talks to the guests, takes pictures, and tries different desserts. Just when Cristina is thinking about leaving the party, fortunately, her boyfriend arrives right on time with the wedding gift and then the two of them can enjoy the rest of the night with peace of mind.

Glosario – Glossary

La boda: the wedding

La prima de Cristina: Cristina's cousin (female)

Le ceremonia en la iglesia: the ceremony at the church

Los invitados: the guests

Una quinta alquilada: a rented villa

Además de: aside from

Los novios: the groom and bride

La familia: the family

Abuela: grandmother

Su abuelo no pudo asistir: her grandfather couldn't come

Está enfermo: he is sick

Conversa: she converses

Está distraída: she is distracted

Hablando: talking

Novio: boyfriend

El encargado de encontrar el regalo: the one in charge of finding the gift

Responsabilidad: responsibility

Él insistió: he insisted

Fue: it was

Las tiendas: the stores

Sábados: Saturdays

La tía: the aunt

Electrodoméstico: appliance

Sería: it would be

Le enseña: she shows her

Licuadoras: blenders

Microondas: microwaves

Batidoras: mixers

Un juego de ollas: a set of pans

El esposo: the husband

Un tostador: a toaster

La madrina: the godmother

Periodista: journalist

Viaja: she travels

El primo: the cousin (male)

Un abogado: a lawyer

Más deudas que dinero: more debt than money

Distraerse: keep herself entertained

Se toma fotos con su sobrina: she takes pictures with her niece

Sobrino: nephew

Charla con su tío: she talks to her uncle

Profesor de filosofía: philosophy professor

Parlanchín: talkative

La vida y el amor: life and love

El centro comercial: the mall

Por favor, apresúrate: please, hurry up

Prueba unos postres de chocolate: she tries some chocolate desserts

Le pregunta al mesero cómo se llaman: she asks the waiter what they are called

No contesta los mensajes: he is not answering her texts

Se siente culpable: she feels guilty

Compró: she bought

Deja todo para último minuto: she leaves everything for the last minute

El nuevo esposo de su prima: her cousin's new husband

Es doctor: he is a doctor

Cirugías: surgeries

Está de vacaciones: he is on vacation

Si todo está bien: if everything is okay

Parece: she seems

Unos zarcillos costosos que le regaló su padrino: some expensive earrings that her godfather gave her

Se siente peor: she feels worse

Lo mejor es irse: the best thing to do is leave

Antes de pasar un momento vergonzoso: before going through an embarrassing moment

Se preparan para cortar el pastel: they are getting ready to cut the cake

Está muy apenado por tardarse tanto: he is very sorry for taking so long

Encontró el regalo ideal: he found the perfect gift

Un reloj de oro: a gold watch

Al fin está relajada: she is relaxed at last

Puede divertirse: she can have fun

Bailar, comer y tomar: to dance, to eat, to drink

Quiere recordar el día con cariño: she wants to remember the day fondly

Ejercicio 1

Contesta las siguientes preguntas – answer the following questions

1- **¿Cómo se llama la iglesia?** – what's the name of the church?

_____

2- **¿Por qué el abuelo de Cristina no pudo asistir a la boda?** – why couldn't Cristina's grandpa attend the wedding?

_____

3- **¿Quién busca el regalo de bodas para Rosa?** – who is looking for Rosa's wedding gift?

_____

4- **¿A qué hora cierran las tiendas los sábados?** – what time do stores close on Saturdays?

_____

5- **¿Qué le regala su madrina cuando vuelve de viaje?** – what does her godmother give her when she's back from her trips?

_____

6- **¿A qué se dedica el tío de Cristina?** – what does Cristina's uncle do?

_____

7- **¿Dónde está el novio de Cristina cuando ella lo llama?** – where's Cristina's boyfriend when she calls him?

_____

8- **¿Qué le pregunta Cristina al mesero?** – what does Cristina ask the waiter?

_____

9- **¿Por qué Cristina se siente culpable?** – why does Cristina feel guilty?

_____

10- **¿Cuál es el regalo?** – what is the present?

_____

Ejercicio 2

Elige entre "verdadero" o "falso" – choose "true" or "false"

1- **La prima de Cristina se llama Rosa.** – Cristina's cousin is called Rosa.

2- **La fiesta es en casa de la novia.** – The party is at the bride's place.

3- **Cristina no ve a su abuela desde hace tres años.** – Cristina hasn't seen her grandma in three years.

4- **Su tía le sugiere que compre un celular como regalo.** – Her aunt suggests she buy a phone as a gift.

5- **El primo de Cristina es un abogado con mucho dinero.** – Cristina's cousin is a wealthy lawyer.

6- **Cristina habla con su tío sobre política.** – Cristina talks to her uncle about politics.

7- **Cristina prueba varios postres de chocolate.** – Cristina tries several chocolate desserts.

8- **El esposo de Rosa es periodista.** – Rosa's husband is a journalist.

9- **Cristina piensa en irse.** – Cristina thinks about leaving.

10- **Cristina se divierte el resto de la noche.** – Cristina has fun the rest of the evening.

Respuestas – Answers

Ejercicio 1

1- La iglesia se llama La Paz de Cristo.

2- El abuelo de Cristina no pudo asistir a la boda porque está enfermo.

3- El novio de Cristina busca el regalo de bodas para Rosa.

4- Las tiendas cierran a las 6 de la tarde los sábados.

5- La madrina de Cristina siempre le regala un perfume nuevo cuando vuelve de viaje.

6- El tío de Cristina es profesor de filosofía.

7- El novio de Cristina está en el centro comercial cuando ella lo llama.

8- Cristina le pregunta al mesero cómo se llaman los postres de chocolate.

9- Cristina se siente culpable porque no compró el reloj con más tiempo.

10- El regalo es un reloj de oro.

Ejercicio 2

1- Verdadero

2- Falso

3- Falso

4- Falso

5- Falso

6- Falso

7- Verdadero

8- Falso

9- Verdadero

10- Verdadero

Puntos clave – Key takeaways

- *La prima de Cristina* is closely translated as "the cousin of Cristina". There's no construction similar to "Cristina's cousin" in Spanish.
- Most professions in Spanish have a masculine and a femenine form (*abogado, abogada*).
- Most adjectives in Spanish have a masculine and a femenine form (*preocupado, preocupada*).
- We usually use the verb *estar* with adjectives that describe feelings.

In the next chapter, you will learn some vocabulary about groceries, how to talk about prices, how to use the verb *haber*, and some partitives in Spanish.

Chapter 4:
Las compras – The grocery shopping

La persona que nunca ha cometido
un error nunca ha hecho nada nuevo.
- Albert Einstein

Omar **suele hacer las compras los domingos**, ya que es mejor porque **no hay tanta gente. Escucha música mientras selecciona qué comprar. Nunca hace una lista**, así que **a menudo se le olvidan algunos artículos**. Se acerca a **la sección de frutas** y **escoge un par de manzanas**. También **hay peras y bananas. No hay**  **fresas ni arándanos, lo cual es una pena** porque las fresas **son sus favoritas. Omar prepara batidos de frutas casi todos los días** y por eso necesita comprar muchas frutas. En **la sección de verduras** hay **tomates jugosos**. También **hay papas, cebollas, pepinos y lechuga**. Hay algunas **zanahorias** pero **están podridas**. Omar le pregunta a **uno de** los trabajadores del supermercado si hay más zanahorias y él **le pide que espere un momento.**

Omar **se pregunta qué más le falta. Aún no busca la leche ni los cereales** ni **el pan.** Él recuerda que el pan aquí es **un poco caro.** Hay **otro lugar** cerca de su casa donde el pan es **más económico**, y a veces hay **buenos descuentos** o **promociones de dos artículos por el precio de uno.** El chico le da a Omar un par de zanahorias **en muy buen estado** y él continúa haciendo sus compras.

Los muslos de pollo están a mitad de precio así que **él se lleva 2 kilos.** Él **ya tiene salmón en su casa** y por eso no compra.

Omar **se encuentra a su vecina.**

—**¿Tú también** compras los domingos? **¿Te falta algo más?**

—No, **creo que solo me falta la pasta y el arroz** —responde Omar.

—**¿Vas a preparar algún platillo especial?**

—No, nada en especial. **¿Y tú?**

—Estoy comprando **los ingredientes** para **el pastel de cumpleaños** de mi hermana. Mañana es su cumpleaños. **Estás invitado.**

—**Gracias**, ¿a qué hora es la fiesta?

—A las 8 de la noche. **Es solo una reunión pequeña.**

—**Bien, nos vemos mañana.**

Hay **dos estantes** con mucho arroz. Él solo necesita **un paquete de 1 kilo.** Toma un paquete y dos paquetes de 1 kilo de pasta, luego se acerca a **la caja** para pagar.

—**¿Eso es todo?** —pregunta el cajero.

—Sí, **por favor.**

—Perfecto, **son 3.500 pesos**.

—**¿Aceptan tarjeta de crédito?**

—Sí, también aceptamos **tarjeta de débito y efectivo**.

En ese momento, Omar se da cuenta que su tarjeta **no está en su bolsillo. Le pide disculpas al cajero** y llama a su novia.

—Creo que **olvidé** mi tarjeta de crédito en la casa.

—**¿En serio?** Yo estoy en casa de mi mamá y **no puedo buscarla**.

—**Sí, lo sé**.

—Bueno, **otro día** haces las compras.

—**No, tranquila, hoy hago todo.**

Omar **está enojado consigo mismo. Se siente como estúpido. Toma un taxi hasta su casa** que **le cobra 200 pesos** y busca su tarjeta. **Pasan algunos minutos y no la encuentra.** No está en **la mesa de noche como él pensaba**, tampoco está en **la mesa del comedor.** Encuentra la tarjeta **encima del refrigerador, lo cual es extraño.** En **media hora** ya está de vuelta en el supermercado. El cajero tiene su **carrito con comida** a su lado. Omar **paga todo** y se va a casa con **las bolsas** de comida.

Resumen

Omar va al supermercado a hacer las compras un domingo. Agarra algunas frutas y verduras mientras intenta recordar qué le falta en casa. Se encuentra a una vecina y conversan por unos minutos. Cuando se dirige a la caja, se da cuenta de que no tiene su tarjeta de débito en el bolsillo y que probablemente la dejó en casa. Con mucha pena, toma un taxi a casa, busca la tarjeta y se devuelve al supermercado para finalmente pagar por sus compras.

Summary

Omar goes to the supermarket to get some groceries on a Sunday. He picks up some fruits and vegetables as he tries to remember what he needs at home. He runs into a neighbor and talks to her for a few minutes. When he gets to the cash register, he realizes he doesn't have his credit card in his pocket, and he probably left it at home. Feeling embarrassed, he takes a taxi home, looks for his card and returns to the supermarket to finally pay for his groceries.

Glosario – Glossary

Suele hacer las compras: he usually goes grocery shopping

Los domingos: on Sundays

No hay tanta gente: there isn't that many people

Escucha música: he listens to music

Mientras selecciona qué comprar: as he selects what to buy

Nunca hace una lista: he never makes a list

A menudo olvida algunos artículos: he often forgets some items

La sección de frutas: the fruit section

Escoge un par de manzanas: he chooses a couple of apples

Hay peras y bananas: there are pears and bananas

No hay fresas ni arándanos: there aren't any strawberries or cranberries

Lo cual es una pena: which is a pity

Son sus favoritas: they are his favorite

Prepara batidos de fruta: he makes smoothies

Casi todos los días: almost every day

La sección de verduras: the vegetable section

Tomates jugosos: juicy tomatoes

Hay papas, cebollas, pepinos y lechuga: there are potatoes, onions, cucumbers, and lettuce

Zanahorias: carrots

Están podridas: they are rotten

Uno de los trabajadores del supermercado: one of the employees of the supermarket

Le pide que espere un minuto: he asks him to wait a minute

Se pregunta qué más le falta: he wonders what else he's missing

Aún no busca la leche ni los cereales: he still hasn't looked for milk or cereals

El pan: the bread

Un poco caro: a bit expensive

Otro lugar: another place

Más económico: cheaper

Buenos descuentos: good discounts

Promociones de dos artículos por el precio de uno: special offers of two items for the price of one

En buen estado: in good shape

Los muslos de pollo: the chicken thighs

Están a mitad de precio: they are half off

Él se lleva 2 kilos: he takes 2 kilograms

Ya tiene salmón en su casa: he already has salmon at home

Se encuentra a su vecina: he runs into his neighbor

Tú también: you too

¿Te falta algo más?: do you need anything else?

Creo que: I think that

Solo me falta la pasta y el arroz: I'm only missing pasta and rice

¿Vas a preparer un plato especial?: Are you going to make a special dish?

¿Y tú?: and you?

Los ingredientes: the ingredients

El pastel de cumpleaños: birthday cake

Estás invitado: you are invited

Gracias: thank you

Es solo una reunión pequeña: it is just a little get-together

Bien, nos vemos mañana: good, see you tomorrow

Dos estantes: two shelves

Un paquete de 1 kilo: a package of 1 kilogram

La caja: the cash register

¿Eso es todo?: is that all?

Por favor: please

Son 3.500 pesos: it is 3,500 pesos

¿Aceptan tarjeta de crédito?: do you take credit cards?

Tarjeta de débito y efectivo: debit card and cash

En ese momento: in that moment

No está en su bolsillo: it is not in his pocket

Le pide disculpas a el cajero: he apologizes to the cashier

(Yo) olvidé: I forgot

¿En serio?: really?

No puedo buscarla: I can't look for it

Sí, lo sé: yes, I know

Otro día: another day

No, tranquila: No, don't worry

Hoy hago todo: I will get it all done today

Está enojado consigo mismo: he is angry at himself

Se siente como estúpido: he feels stupid

Toma un taxi hasta su casa: he takes a taxi home

Le cobra 200 pesos: he charges him 200 pesos

Pasan algunos minutos: a few minutes go by

No la encuentra: he can't find it

La mesa de noche: the nightstand

Como él pensaba: as he thought

La mesa del comedor: the dining table

Encima del refrigerador: on the fridge

Lo cual es extraño: which is weird

Media hora: half an hour

Carrito con comida: shopping cart with food

Paga todo: he pays for everything

Las bolsas: the bags

Ejercicio 1

Contesta las siguientes preguntas – answer the following questions

1- ¿Por qué Omar hace las compras los domingos? – why does Omar do the grocery shopping on Sundays?

_____

2- ¿Cuál es la fruta favorita de Omar? – what 's Omar' s favorite fruit?

_____

3- ¿Qué verduras hay en la sección de verduras? – what vegetables are there in the vegetable section?

_____

4- ¿Por qué Omar no compra pan ahí? – why doesn't Omar buy bread there?

_____

5- ¿Cuántos kilos de muslo de pollo compra Omar? – how many kilograms of chicken thighs does Omar buy?

_____

6- ¿Qué compra su vecina? – what is his neighbor buying?

_____

7- ¿A qué hora es la fiesta de la hermana de la vecina? – what time is his neighbor's sister's party?

_____

8- ¿Por qué Omar no puede pagar su comida? – why can't Omar pay for his food?

_____

9- ¿Cuánto le cobra el taxi a casa? – how much is the taxi home?

_____

10- ¿Dónde está la tarjeta de crédito? – where is his credit card?

_____

Ejercicio 2

Elige entre "verdadero" o "falso" – choose "true" or "false"

1- **Omar nunca olvida ningún artículo.** – Omar never forgets any items.

_____

2- **No hay bananas en la sección de frutas.** – There are no bananas in the fruit section.

_____

3- **Las zanahorias están podridas.** – The carrots are rotten.

_____

4- **Omar compra 1 kilo de salmón.** – Omar buys 1 kilogram of salmon.

_____

5- **Omar rechaza la invitación de su vecina.** – Omar turns down his neighbor's invitation.

_____

6- **Omar compra 2 kilos de pasta.** – Omar buys 2 kilograms of pasta.

_____

7- **El total de Omar es 4.000 pesos.** – Omar's total is 4,000 pesos.

_____

8- **Omar toma un taxi a casa.** – Omar takes a taxi home.

_____

9- **Omar tiene que buscar los artículos de nuevo.** – Omar has to look for the food items again.

_____

10- **Omar paga en efectivo.** – Omar pays in cash.

_____

Respuestas – Answers

Ejercicio 1

1- Omar hace las compras los domingos porque no hay tanta gente.

2- La fresa es la fruta favorita de Omar.

3- En la sección de verduras hay tomates, papas, cebollas, pepinos, lechuga y zanahorias.

4- Omar no compra pan ahí porque es un poco caro.

5- Omar compra 2 kilos de muslo de pollo.

6- La vecina de Omar compra los ingredientes para el pastel de cumpleaños de su hermana.

7- La fiesta de la hermana de la vecina es a las 8 de la noche.

8- Omar no puede pagar su comida porque no tiene su tarjeta de crédito.

9- El taxi a casa le cobra 200 pesos.

10- La tarjeta de crédito está encima del refrigerador.

Ejercicio 2

1- Falso

2- Falso

3- Verdadero

4- Falso

5- Falso

6- Verdadero

7- Falso

8- Verdadero

9- Falso

10- Falso

Puntos clave – Key takeaways

- When we talk about prices, we say *son* followed by the price, "*son 100 pesos*".
- The verb *soler* is often translated as the adverb usually, and it's always followed by another verb.
- *Hay* can be translated as either "there is" or "there are".

In the next chapter, you will learn some vocabulary about school supplies, colors, how to use plural nouns, and how to ask and give personal information.

Chapter 5:
De vuelta a clases – Back to classes

Una buena madre vale por cien maestros.
- George Herbert

El hijo de Marisol **empieza las clases en un par de días.** Este año **está en segundo grado.** Marisol **le pide a su hermana que la acompañe** a una tienda a comprar algunas cosas para su hijo. Escoge unos nuevos **cuadernos,** unos muy hermosos. **Está segura de que su hijo va a estar feliz con** los cuadernos de **super héroes. Su color favorito es el rojo,** así que compra uno rojo, también uno **amarillo,** uno **azul** y uno **verde.** Todos con **colores** lindos. **Por desgracia,** Marisol **no consigue todos los libros** de su hijo en esta tienda. Solo puede comprar el libro de **historia** y el libro de **matemáticas.**

Le preocupa un poco porque las tiendas cierran en una hora, pero espera encontrar el resto de los útiles escolares pronto. En una tienda de computadoras y celulares pregunta el precio de algunos artículos. Hay una computadora muy moderna que quiere comprar pero no tiene suficiente dinero. Ve un celular a buen precio y piensa en su hijo. Él está creciendo y necesita un celular para comunicarse. Marisol decide comprarlo con la tarjeta de crédito.

–Necesito algunos datos para finalizar su compra.

–Está bien, no hay problema –responde Marisol.

–¿Cuál es su número de teléfono?

–Mi número de teléfono es 0 11 25184567.

–Muy bien, ¿cuál es su correo electrónico?

–Marisol@gmail.com

–Por último, ¿cuál es su estado civil?

–¿En verdad necesita esa información?

–Sí, es una de las preguntas estándares.

–Okey, estoy soltera.

–Aquí tiene, que disfrute su compra.

Marisol y su hermana salen de la tienda y se apresuran a buscar las cosas que les faltan. En media hora cierran las tiendas.

–Esas preguntas fueron muy extrañas, ¿no te parece? – pregunta Marisol.

–Sí, no entiendo por qué necesita saber si estás casada o no.

Marisol busca en los estantes de libros en otra tienda. Hay libros de castellano y literatura de primer grado hasta sexto grado. Marisol agarra el libro de segundo grado y también compra los libros de **física y química** para Anabel, **su hija mayor**.

–¿Te falta **lápiz y borra**? –pregunta su hermana.

–Sí, **agarra una caja de lápices y dos borras**.

–**Mira esta cartuchera. Está muy linda**.

–Sí, es linda. **¿Cuánto cuesta?**

–600 pesos.

–Está bien. También **necesito comprar una caja de colores**.

Marisol **gasta** casi 3000 pesos en todos los artículos. El hombre **le entrega** las cosas y ellas se van.

–**¿Qué te falta?** –pregunta su hermana.

–Solo falta **el uniforme**, **la camisa blanca** y **el pantalón azul oscuro**.

Cuando llegan a **la tienda donde venden ropa escolar, las puertas están cerradas**.

–¿**Ya cerraron**?

–Sí, **ya cerramos por hoy** –dice **el dueño de la tienda**.

–Tengo que comprar el uniforme de mi hijo.

–**Disculpe, vuelva mañana**.

Marisol y su hermana **toman el tren** a su casa. Marisol **se siente un poco desanimada** porque no compró el uniforme de su hijo.

–**No te preocupes**, lo compras mañana –dice su hermana.

–Mañana no puedo, **estoy ocupada todo el día** en la oficina.

–**Yo sé que encontrarás una manera de hacerlo**.

–**Eso espero**.

–¿La computadora es para Anabel?

–Sí, este año estudia **computación** y necesita **una mejor computadora**.

–Pero esas computadoras **están carísimas**.

–Sí, **tengo que pensarlo. Puedo pedir un préstamo en el banco**.

Antes de ir a casa, Marisol toma una taza de café en casa de su hermana. El esposo de su hermana la saluda y **le pregunta cómo están sus hijos**. Cuando Marisol le habla sobre el uniforme de su hijo Carlos, **él se ofrece a comprar** el uniforme porque **tiene el día libre**. Marisol le agradece y se siente más aliviada. Habla con ellos **por casi una hora** y luego se va a casa **a descansar**.

Resumen

Marisol va a varias tiendas a comprar los útiles escolares de sus hijos en compañía de su hermana. Compra cuadernos, libros, lápices, cartucheras y otros artículos, incluso un celular para su hijo más pequeño. Tiene muy poco tiempo así que se apresura yendo de tienda en tienda. Por desgracia, la tienda de uniformes escolares está cerrada cuando llega y no puede comprar la camisa blanca y el pantalón azul oscuro que su hijo necesita. Algo desanimada, se detiene en casa de su hermana a tomar café. Luego de hablar con el esposo de su hermana, él se ofrece a comprar el uniforme de su hijo, resolviendo su problema.

Summary

Marisol goes to a few stores to get her kids' school supplies along with her sister. She buys notebooks, books, pencils, pencil cases and other items, even a phone for her younger son. She has very little time so she has to hurry as she makes her way from store to store. Unfortunately, the uniform store is already closed when she gets there so she can't buy the white shirt and dark blue pants her son needs. Feeling a bit down, she stops at her sister's for some coffee. After talking to her sister's husband, he offers to buy her son's uniform, solving her problems.

Glosario – Glossary

Empieza las clases: he starts classes

En un par de días: in a couple of days

Está en segundo grado: he is in second grade

Le pide a su hermana que la acompañe: she asks her sister to come with her

Cuadernos: notebooks

Está segura de que su hijo va a estar feliz con: she is sure her son is going to be happy with

Super héroes: he never makes a list

Su color favorito es el rojo: his favorite color is red

Amarillo, azul y verde: yellow, blue, and green

Por desgracia: unfortunately

No consigue todos los libros: she can't find all the books

Historia: history

Matemáticas: math

Le preocupa: it worries her

Las tiendas cierran: the stores close

Espera encontrar el resto de los útiles escolares: she hopes to find the rest of the school supplies

Computadoras y celulares: computers and cell phones

El precio: the price

Moderna: modern

Quiere comprar: she wants to buy

No tiene suficiente dinero: she doesn't have enough money

A buen precio: at a good price

Él está creciendo: he is growing up

Necesita: he needs

Para comunicarse: to keep in touch

Decide comprarlo: she decides to buy it

Algunos datos para finalizar su compra: some information to complete your purchase

Está bien: that's okay

¿Cuál es su número de teléfono?: what's your phone number?

¿Cuál es su correo electrónico?: what's your email address?

(@) arroba: at

(.) punto: dot

Por último: lastly

¿Cuál es su estado civil?: what's your marital status?

Esa información: that information

Preguntas estándares: standard questions

Okey: okay

Estoy soltera: I am single

Aquí tiene: here you go

Que disfrute su compra: enjoy your purchase

Salen: they leave

Las cosas que les faltan: the rest of the things they need

Fueron muy extrañas: they were very strange

¿No te parece?: don't you think?

No entiendo por qué: I don't understand why

Necesita saber si estás casada o no: he needs to know if you're married or not

Castellano y literatura: Spanish and literature

Primer grado: first grade

Sexto grado: sixth grade

Física y química: physics and chemistry

Su hija mayor: her eldest daughter

Lápiz y borra: a pencil and an eraser

Agarra: take

Una caja de lápices: a box of pencils

Dos borras: two erasers

Mira esta cartuchera: look at this pencil case

Está muy linda: it is really pretty

¿Cuánto cuesta?: how much does it cost?

Necesito comprar una caja de colores: I need to buy a box of colored pencils

Gasta: she spends

Le entrega: he gives her

¿Qué te falta?: what else do you need?

El uniforme: the uniform

La camisa blanca: the white shirt

El pantalón azul oscuro: the dark blue pants

La tienda donde venden ropa escolar: the store where they sell school uniforms

Las puertas están cerradas: the doors are closed

¿Ya cerraron?: are you closed?

Ya cerramos por hoy: we are closed for the day

El dueño de la tienda: the store's owner

Disculpe, vuelva mañana: I'm sorry, come back tomorrow

Toman el tren: they take the train

Se siente un poco desanimada: she feels a bit down

No te preocupes: don't worry

Estoy ocupada todo el día: I will be busy all day

Yo sé que encontrarás una manera de hacerlo: I know you will find a way to do it

Eso espero: I hope so

Computación: IT

Una mejor computadora: a better computer

Están carísimas: they are extremely expensive

Tengo que pensarlo: I have to think about it

Puedo pedir un préstamo en el banco: I can get a loan from the bank

Le pregunta cómo están sus hijos: he asks her how her kids are

Él se ofrece a comprar: he offers to buy

Tiene el día libre: he has the day off

Por casi una hora: for almost an hour

A descansar: to rest

Ejercicio 1

Contesta las siguientes preguntas – answer the following questions

1- **¿Quién acompaña a Marisol?** – who is accompanying Marisol?

_____

2- **¿De qué colores son los cuadernos que compra Marisol?** – what color are the notebooks Marisol buys?

_____

3- **¿Qué libros compra en la primera tienda?** – what books does she buy in the first store?

_____

4- **¿Por qué Marisol no compra la computadora?** – why doesn't Marisol buy the computer?

_____

5- **¿Marisol está casada?** – Is Marisol married?

_____

6- **¿Qué piensa Marisol de las preguntas del empleado de la tienda?** – what does Marisol think about the store employee's questions?

_____

7- **¿Qué libros compra Marisol para su hija?** – what books does Marisol buy for her daughter?

_____

8- ¿Por qué Marisol no puede comprar el uniforme de su hijo? – why can't Marisol buy her son's uniform?

_____

9- ¿Por qué Anabel necesita una nueva computadora? – why does Anabel need a new computer?

_____

10- ¿Quién se ofrece a comprar el uniforme? – who offers to buy the uniform?

_____

Ejercicio 2

Elige entre "verdadero" o "falso" – choose "true" or "false"

1- **El hijo de Marisol está en tercer grado.** – Marisol's son is in third grade.

_____

2- **El color favorito del hijo de Marisol es el rojo.** – Marisol's son's favorite color is red.

_____

3- **Las tiendas cierran en dos horas.** – The stores close in two hours.

_____

4- **Marisol se compra un celular para sí misma.** – Marisol buys a phone for herself.

_____

5- **Marisol está soltera.** – Marisol is single.

_____

6- **Marisol gasta casi 3.000 pesos en una de las tiendas.** – Marisol spends almost 3,000 pesos in one of the stores.

_____

7- **Marisol tiene que comprar una camisa azul.** – Marisol has to buy a blue shirt.

_____

8- **Marisol toma un autobús a casa.** – Marisol takes the bus home.

9- **Marisol considera pedir un préstamo al banco.** – Marisol is considering getting a loan from the bank.

10- **Marisol se toma un café en casa de su hermana.** – Marisol has a coffee at her sister's.

Respuestas – Answers

Ejercicio 1

1- La hermana de Marisol la acompaña.

2- Marisol compra un cuaderno rojo, uno amarillo, uno azul y uno verde.

3- Marisol compra el libro de historia y el de matemáticas.

4- Marisol no compra la computadora porque no tiene suficiente dinero.

5- No, Marisol está soltera.

6- Marisol piensa que las preguntas del empleado de la tienda son extrañas.

7- Marisol compra un libro de física y uno de química para su hija.

8- Marisol no puede comprar el uniforme de su hijo porque cuando llega a la tienda ya está cerrada.

9- Anabel necesita una nueva computadora porque este año estudia computación.

10- El esposo de la hermana de Marisol se ofrece a comprar el uniforme.

Ejercicio 2

1- Falso

2- Verdadero

3- Falso

4- Falso

5- Verdadero

6- Verdadero

7- Falso

8- Falso

9- Verdadero

10- Verdadero

Puntos clave – Key takeaways

- Most adjectives in Spanish have a singular and a plural form (*lindo, lindos*).
- Nouns that end in a vowel can be turned into plural by adding an *s* (*cuaderno = cuadernos*).
- Nouns that end in a consonant can be turned into plural by adding *es* (*color = colores*).
- *¿Cuánto cuesta?* or *¿Cuánto es?* are questions to ask about prices.

In the next chapter, you will learn how to use the verb *gustar*, some adjectives to describe both appearance and personality, and how to make comparisons between two people.

Chapter 6:
La cita – The date

No hay ningún instinto como el del corazón.
- Lord Byron

Daniela está soltera y **a Cristina le encanta presentarle chicos nuevos.** Aunque son muy **buenas amigas,** Cristina **no sabe muy bien qué tipo de hombres le gustan a Daniela,** y **por eso las citas** siempre son **un completo desastre. Para evitar esos momentos incó-modos,** Daniela **descargó una aplicación de citas** llamada **Cupido para encontrar** a **un chico que a ella le parezca interesante.** Ella **no sabe si quiere una relación** o **algo**  **más casual. De momento, la idea es divertirse.**

Cristina y Daniela **se juntan** para ver los distintos **perfiles de los chicos** y ven **algunos más interesantes que otros.** Hay muchos perfiles **con pocas fotos,** otros **sin ninguna** descripción ni información sobre el posible candidato. Ellas **descartan** este tipo de perfiles inmediatamente. A Daniela le gustan **los hombres que se toman el tiempo para al menos describirse un poco**. También encuentran algunos chicos muy **apuestos y encantadores**. **Entre esos** chicos, **hay dos que a Daniela le encantan**: uno es un chico llamado Juan y el otro se llama Sebastián.

Juan es abogado, **lo cual no le gusta a Cristina** porque piensa que **significa que Juan es aburrido**. Pero a Daniela le gusta que Juan **tenga un lado creativo**. Juan **dice que le gusta cantar y escribir poemas. Parece que** Juan es un chico **sensible, lo cual es bueno para Daniela**. Juan dice que es un chico **introvertido**, que **prefiere quedarse en casa viendo una película que salir a un bar a tomar**. A Daniela le gusta ver películas en casa, pero también **le gusta salir** y **le gustaría** salir con Juan **de vez en cuando**, entonces **no sabe si sus personalidades son compatibles**.

Sebastián es dos años menor que Daniela y **estudia economía. Por el momento** no trabaja y **sus padres lo ayudan económicamente**. Daniela prefiere a hombres que son **independientes**, pero Sebastián tiene **otras cualidades buenas**. Le gusta mucho cocinar y parece muy **atento**. También le gusta salir a **explorar nuevos lugares**, tiene muchas fotos en **montañas**, diferentes **playas, andando en bicicleta**. A Daniela le gustan las **actividades al aire libre** y le parece que sus personalidades **pueden ser** compatibles.

Juan es **cinco años mayor que** Sebastián, y también es **más alto**. Sebastián es **más musculoso que** Juan y también es **más extrovertido y directo**. Sebastián parece **menos maduro que** Juan, pero **Sebastián es tan educado como Juan**. Daniela cree que Juan es **más apuesto** que Sebastián, pero Juan **coquetea mejor** que Sebastián.

Sebastián **vive más lejos** que Juan, lo cual puede ser un problema si Daniela quiere **hacer planes con él**. A Juan **le gustan los animales** y a Sebastián no, y Daniela tiene un **gato** así que **quizás eso sea** un problema.

Daniela está muy **indecisa**.

—**¿Quién te gusta más?** —pregunta Cristina.

—**La verdad**, no sé. **Ambos** tienen buenas y **malas** cualidades.

—**A ti te gustan** los chicos **graciosos. ¿Quién es más gracioso?**

—Creo que Sebastián es más gracioso que Juan.

—¿Juan es **más atractivo** que Sebastián?

—Ambos son muy lindos.

—¿Quién es **más respetuoso**?

—Creo que Juan.

—**¿Quién es menos atento?**

—Creo que Sebastián.

—¿Juan es **más listo** que Sebastián?

—No, creo que Sebastián es **tan inteligente como** Juan. Es una decisión muy difícil.

En los siguientes días, Daniela tiene una cita con los dos chicos. El jueves Daniela **va al cine** con Juan, y el sábado va a un bar con Sebastián. El domingo en la mañana, Daniela ve a Cristina y **le cuenta todo**.

—¿Ya sabes quién te gusta más? —pregunta Cristina.

—**Estoy más confundida que nunca** —responde Daniela.

—¿Por qué?

—Creo que **los dos me gustan igual**. Juan es muy **caballeroso**, y también **es buen besador**. Sebastián **es bueno bailando** y la paso muy bien con él, y se nota que tiene un lado sensible. ¿Qué hago?

–Pues, conócelos un poco mejor, y con el tiempo decide qué vas a hacer. De momento, disfruta de su compañía. No tienes que apresurarte.

–Tienes toda la razón, es muy temprano para tomar una decisión. Gracias por tus consejos.

Resumen

Daniela está buscando conocer chicos interesantes, así que descarga una aplicación de citas llamada Cupido. Su amiga Cristina le ayuda a revisar los perfiles de muchos chicos y a escoger los mejores para tener una cita. Entre tantos perfiles, encuentran a dos chicos que parecen prometedores: Juan y Sebastián. Daniela y Cristina hablan sobre los atributos de ambos chicos y si creen que serían compatibles con Daniela. Más tarde esa semana, Daniela tiene una cita con cada uno de los chicos, y al final ella decide que quiere ir conociéndolos sin prisa.

Summary

Daniela is looking to meet interesting guys so she downloads a dating app called Cupid. Her friend Cristina helps her check the profiles and choose the best ones to go on a date with. Among all the profiles, they find two guys that seem promising: Juan and Sebastián. Daniela and Cristina talk about the attributes of both guys and whether they think they would be a good match with Daniela. Later that week, Daniela has a date with each of the guys, and in the end she decides she wants to get to know them in no rush.

Glosario – Glossary

A Cristina le encanta presentarle chicos nuevos: Cristina loves to introduce new guys to her

Buenas amigas: good friends

No sabe muy bien: she doesn't know that well

Qué tipo de hombres le gustan a Daniela: what type of men Daniela likes

Por eso: that's why

Las citas: the dates

Un completo desastre: a total disaster

Para evitar: to avoid

Esos momentos incómodos: those awkward moments

Descargó una aplicación de citas: she downloaded a dating app

Cupido: Cupid

Para encontrar: to find

Un chico que a ella le parezca interesante: a guy she finds interesting

No sabe si quiere: she doesn't know if she wants

Una relación: a relationship

Algo más casual: something more casual

De momento: for the time being

La idea es divertirse: the idea is to have fun

Se juntan: they get together

Los perfiles de los chicos: the guys' profiles

Algunos más interesantes que otros: some more interesting than others

Con pocas fotos: with few pictures

Sin ninguna descripción ni información: with no description or information

Sobre el posible candidato: about the possible candidate

Descartan: they rule out

Los hombres que se toman el tiempo: the men who take the time

Para al menos describirse un poco: to at least describe themselves a bit

Apuestos y encantadores: handsome and charming

Entre esos: among those

Hay dos que a Daniela le encantan: there are two that Daniela loves

Lo cual no le gusta a Cristina: which Cristina doesn't like

Significa que: it means

Juan es aburrido: Juan is boring

Tiene un lado creativo: he has a creative side

Dice que le gusta cantar y escribir poemas: he says he likes to sing and to write poems

Parece que: it seems that

Sensible: tender

Lo cual es bueno para Daniela: which is good for Daniela

Introvertido: introverted

Prefiere: he prefers

Quedarse en casa viendo una película: to stay home watching a movie

Que salir a un bar a tomar: rather than going out to a bar to drink

Le gusta salir: she likes to go out

Le gustaría: she would like

De vez en cuando: once in a while

No sabe si: she doesn't know if

Sus personalidades son compatibles: their personalities are compatible

Sebastián es dos años menor que Daniela: Sebastián is two years younger than Daniela

Estudia economía: he studies economics

Por el momento: for the moment

Sus padres lo ayudan: his parents help him

Económicamente: financially

Independientes: independent

Otras cualidades buenas: other good qualities

Atento: thoughtful

Explorar nuevos lugares: to explore new places

Montañas: mountains

Playas: beaches

Manejando bicicleta: riding a bike

Actividades al aire libre: outdoor activities

Pueden ser: they might be

Cinco años mayor que: five years older than

Más alto: taller

Más musculoso que: more muscular than

Más extrovertido y directo: more extroverted and direct

Menos maduro que: less mature than

Sebastián es tan educado como Juan: Sebastián is as polite as Juan

Más apuesto: more handsome

Coquetea mejor: he flirts better

Vive más lejos: he lives farther

Hacer planes con él: to make plans with him

Le gustan los animales: he likes animals

Gatos: cats

Quizás eso sea: that might be

Indecisa: indecisive

¿Quién te gusta más?: who do you like more?

La verdad: honestly

Ambos: they both

Malas: bad

A ti te gustan: you like

Graciosos: funny

¿Quién es más gracioso?: who is funnier?

Más atractivo: more attractive

Más respetuoso: more respectful

¿Quién es menos atento?: who is less thoughtful?

Más listo: smarter

Tan inteligente como: as smart as

En los siguientes días: in the following days

Va al cine: she goes to the movies

Le cuenta todo: she tells her everything

Estoy más confundida que nunca: I'm more confused than ever before

Los dos me gustan igual: I like them both the same

Caballeroso: chivalrous

Es buen besador: he is a good kisser

Es bueno bailando: he is a great dancer

La paso muy bien con él: I have a great time with him

Se nota que tiene un lado sensible: you can tell he has a sensitive side

¿Qué hago?: what should I do?

Pues, conócelos un poco mejor: Well, get to know them a little better

Con el tiempo: with time

Decide qué vas a hacer: decide what you're going to do

Disfruta de su compañía: enjoy their company

No tienes que apresurarte: you don't have to rush

Tienes toda la razón: you're totally right

Es muy temprano: it's too early

Para tomar una decisión: to make a decision

Consejos: advice

Ejercicio 1

Contesta las siguientes preguntas – answer the following questions

1- ¿Por qué sus citas son tan malas? – why are her dates so bad?

_____

2- ¿Qué es Cupido? – what is Cupid?

_____

3- ¿Qué busca Daniela ahora? – what is Daniela looking for right now?

_____

4- ¿Qué tipo de perfiles no le gustan a Daniela? – what kinds of profiles doesn't Daniela like?

_____

5- ¿Por qué a Cristina no le gusta que Juan sea abogado? – why doesn't Cristina like Juan being a lawyer?

_____

6- ¿Cuál es el lado creativo de Juan? – what is Juan's creative side?

_____

7- ¿Juan es sociable? – is Juan sociable?

_____

8- **¿Cómo paga sus cuentas Sebastián?** – how does Sebastián pay his bills?

_____

9- **¿Por qué Daniela piensa que ella y Sebastián son compatibles?** – why does Daniela think that she and Sebastián are compatible?

_____

10- **¿Qué piensa hacer Daniela al final?** – what is Daniela considering in the end?

_____

Ejercicio 2

Elige entre "verdadero" o "falso" – choose "true" or "false"

1- **Daniela y Cristina son primas.** – Daniela and Cristina are cousins.

_____

2- **A Daniela le gusta el lado creativo de Juan.** – Daniela likes Juan's creative side.

_____

3- **Sebastián es menor que Daniela.** – Sebastián is younger than Daniela.

_____

4- **Sebastián es más alto que Juan.** – Sebastián is taller than Juan.

_____

5- **A Juan no le gustan los animales.** – Juan doesn't like animals.

_____

6- **Juan es más atento que Sebastián.** – Juan is more thoughtful than Sebastián.

_____

7- **Daniela va al cine con Juan.** – Daniela goes to the movies with Juan.

_____

8- **Daniela ve a Cristina el sábado a la noche.** – Daniela meets Cristina on Saturday night.

9- **Sebastián es bueno bailando.** – Sebastián is a good dancer.

10- **Daniela comienza una relación con Juan.** – Daniela starts a relationship with Juan.

Respuestas – Answers

Ejercicio 1

1- Las citas de Daniela son malas porque su amiga no sabe el tipo de hombre que le gusta.

2- Cupido es una aplicación de citas.

3- Por ahora, Daniela busca divertirse.

4- A Daniela no le gustan los perfiles sin fotos o con poca información.

5- A Cristina no le gusta que Juan sea abogado porque piensa que puede ser aburrido.

6- El lado creativo de Juan es que le gusta cantar y escribir.

7- No, Juan es un poco introvertido.

8- Los padres de Sebastián lo ayudan económicamente.

9- Daniela piensa que ella y Sebastián son compatibles porque a ambos les gustan las actividades al aire libre.

10- Daniela piensa conocer mejor a Juan y a Sebastián, sin apresurarse.

Ejercicio 2

1- Falso

2- Verdadero

3- Verdadero

4- Falso

5- Falso

6- Verdadero

7- Verdadero

8- Falso

9- Verdadero

10- Falso

Puntos clave – Key takeaways

- The verb *gustar* is very particular. *Me gusta el café* can be closely translated as "coffee pleases me".
- When we use verbs like *gustar*, we have to switch the structure of the sentence around. Though *me gusta el café* means "I like coffee", here *el café* is the subject of the sentence, unlike in English where "coffee" is the object of the sentence.
- *Gustar* is preceded by the correct objective pronoun (*me, te, le, nos, les*).
- To make comparisons we use *más* an adjective and *que*, (*Yo soy más alto que tú* = I'm taller than you)

In the next chapter, you will learn vocabulary about parts of the house, adverbs of place, and how to talk about possession.

Chapter 7:
El gatito – The kitten

El tiempo pasado en compañía de gatos
no es tiempo malgastado.
- Sigmund Freud

Daniela vive en una casa **antigua** en Belgrano, un **barrio algo costoso** en la ciudad de Buenos Aires. A ella le gustaría vivir **sola**, pero, **por desgracia,** necesita a sus dos **compañeras de piso** para **compartir los gastos del alquiler. Ella y Raquel se llevan muy bien.** Tienen algunas **cosas en común** y a menudo **hablan sobre su día** o **alguna otra cosa que tengan en mente.** Raquel es muy **trabajadora y ordenada**, y también es **servicial.**

Ayuda con **la limpieza de la casa** y en ocasiones **le prepara el almuerzo o la cena** a Daniela.

Martina es **un caso diferente. Constantemente está de muy mal humor**, y **casi nunca** ayuda con las cosas de la casa. Su **habitación** siempre es un desastre y no es **considerada** ni con Daniela ni con Raquel. A veces **incluso es maleducada**, ya que **ignora a Daniela** cuando **le hace alguna pregunta. Tanto Daniela como Raquel odian a Martina.**

Daniela **adoptó un gatito** recientemente. A Raquel **le gustó la idea de una mascota**, y Martina **no dio su opinión.** El gatito es hermoso, **de pelaje negro** y **ojos marrones.** A menudo **llora mucho porque quiere comida** o porque **quiere dormir. Eso es lo que hace** el gatito **todo el día.** Duerme, come y llora. También **le gusta esconderse en lugares extraños.**

El gatito está desaparecido desde esta mañana.

—**No te voy a ayudar a buscarlo. Es tu gato, no el mío** – dijo Martina.

Daniela **no le hace caso** y **sigue buscando al gato.**

—¿Está **detrás del mueble?** –pregunta Raquel.

—**No, ahí no está** –responde Daniela.

Busca **debajo de la cama** pero solo ve unos **tacones rojos.**

—**¿De quién son estos tacones?** –pregunta Daniela.

—**Son míos** –responde Raquel.

Entre la cama y la mesa de noche, Daniela encuentra unos **audífonos blancos.**

—¿Estos audífonos son **tuyos**, Raquel?

—No, no son míos. ¿Y Martina? Tal vez son **suyos.**

—Sí, **supongo que son de ella.**

Las chicas están preocupadas porque no encuentran al gato **aún. Le sirven un poco de leche** en un plato **para atraerlo**, pero

no funciona. Siguen buscando en todos los lugares **que se les ocurre** que **el gatito pueda estar**. **Encima de la nevera** no está, tampoco en el pequeño espacio **junto a la planta de sábila**. Raquel cree que el gatito puede estar **dentro de las cajas vacías** en su cuarto, ya que **le gusta jugar ahí**, pero no lo encuentran.

—**¿Qué importa? Adopta** otro gato —dice Martina

Daniela y Raquel ignoran **sus comentarios**.

Daniela **cancela su clase de yoga** para seguir buscando al gatito. **Todavía tiene esperanzas de encontrarlo. A eso de las 8 p.m.**, Daniela **escucha un sonido** y le pregunta a Raquel **si ella también lo escucha**. Las dos **siguen el sonido** hasta el baño, **parece venir del cesto de la ropa sucia. Mueven el cesto** y ven al gatito. Las dos **casi lloran de la emoción**, están muy **contentas** porque al fin **encontraron** al gatito. Piensan que el gato **tiene mucha hambre** así que le dan algo de leche, y, como **se la toma muy rápido**, le dan un poco más. Daniela le prepara una **pequeña camita para que duerma** en el cuarto con ella.

Al día siguiente, Martina le dice a Daniela que tiene algo **para ella**. Le da una bolsa y **dentro de ella** hay **un collar con cascabel** para el gatito.

—**¿Y eso que compraste esto?** —pregunta Daniela.

—Bueno, **ayer estaban preocupadas por el estúpido gato** así que **me parece que** ese collar **puede ayudar a que lo encuentren la próxima vez**.

—**Es precioso. ¿Dónde lo compraste?** —pregunta Raquel.

—En **la tienda de mascotas** que está **enfrente de mi oficina**.

—**Es un lindo detalle**, gracias —dice Daniela.

Daniela y Raquel **están sorprendidas** con **la actitud de Martina hacia el gato desde ese momento.** Tal vez **no es tan mala persona como ellas pensaban.**

Resumen

Daniela adoptó a un gatito recientemente. Por desgracia, el gatito se pierde y Daniela no puede encontrarlo en ningún lado. Raquel, su compañera de piso, la ayuda a buscar al gatito. Su otra compañera, Martina, no ayuda en nada. Es evidente que no le importa el gato, y esto es solo una de las razones por las que Raquel y Daniela odian a Martina. Se la pasan todo el día buscando al gato pero no pueden encontrarlo. No es hasta las 8 de la noche que al fin lo encuentran detrás del cesto de ropa sucia en el baño. Al día siguiente, Martina le compra un collar de cascabel al gato luego de ver lo preocupadas que estaban sus compañeras, lo que hace que Daniela y Raquel cambien un poco su opinión sobre ella.

Summary

Daniela adopted a kitten recently. Unfortunately, the cat is missing and Daniela can't find it anywhere. Raquel, her roommate, helps her look for the kitten. Her other roommate, Martina, doesn't help at all. It's clear she doesn't care about the cat, and this is just one of the reasons why Raquel and Daniela hate Martina. They spend all day looking for the cat but they can't find it. It's not until 8 at night that they finally find the cat behind the laundry hamper in the bathroom. The next day, Martina buys a collar with a bell for the cat after seeing how worried her roommates were, which makes Daniela and Raquel change their mind about her a little.

Glosario – Glossary

Antigua: ancient

Barrio: neighborhood

Algo costoso: somewhat expensive

Sola: alone

Por desgracia: unfortunately

Compañeras de piso: roommates

Compartir los gastos del alquiler: to share the rent

Ella y Raquel se llevan muy bien: she and Raquel get along pretty well

Cosas en común: things in common

Hablan sobre su día: they talk about their day

Alguna otra cosa que tengan en mente: any other thing they have in mind

Trabajadora y ordenada: hardworking and organized

Servicial: helpful

La limpieza de la casa: the house chores

Le prepara el almuerzo o la cena: she makes lunch or dinner for her

Un caso diferente: a different case

Constantemente: constantly

Está de muy mal humor: she's in a very bad mood

Casi nunca: almost never

Habitación: bedroom

Considerada: considerate

Incluso es maleducada: she's even rude

Ignora a Daniela: she ignores Daniela

Le hace alguna pregunta: she asks her a question

Tanto Daniela como Raquel odian a Martina: both Daniela and Raquel hate Martina

Adoptó un gatito: she adopted a cat

Le gustó la idea de una mascota: she liked the idea of a pet

No dio su opinión: she didn't give her opinion

De pelaje negro: with black fur

Ojos marrones: brown eyes

Llora mucho porque quiere comida: he cries a lot because he wants food

Quiere dormir: he wants to sleep

Eso es lo que hace: that's what he does

Todo el día: all day

Le gusta esconderse en lugares extraños: he likes to hide in strange places

El gatito está desaparecido desde esta mañana: the kitten has been missing since this morning

No te voy a ayudar a buscarlo: I'm not going to help you look for him

Es tu gato, no el mío: it's your cat, not mine

No le hace caso: she doesn't listen to her

Sigue buscando al gato: she keeps looking for the cat

Detrás del mueble: behind the couch

No, ahí no está: no, he's not there

Debajo de la cama: under the bed

Tacones rojos: red high heels

¿De quién son estos tacones?: whose high heels are these?

Son míos: they're mine

Entre la cama y la mesa de noche: between the bed and the nightstand

Audífonos blancos: white earphones

Tuyos: yours

Suyos: hers

Supongo que son de ella: I guess they're hers

Aún: yet

Le sirven un poco de leche: they pour him some milk

Para atraerlo: to lure him

Que se les ocurre: that they can think of

El gatito pueda estar: the kitten may be

Encima de la nevera: on the refrigerator

Junto a la planta de sábila: next to the aloe vera plant

Dentro de las cajas vacías: inside the empty boxes

Le gusta jugar ahí: he likes to play there

¿Qué importa?: who cares?

Adopta: adopt (imperative)

Sus comentarios: her comments

Cancela su clase de yoga: she cancels her yoga class

Todavía tiene esperanzas de encontrarlo: she still has hopes of finding him

A eso de las 8 p.m.: at around 8 p.m.

Escucha un sonido: she hears a sound

Si ella también lo escucha: if she hears it too

Siguen el sonido: they follow the sound

Parece venir del cesto de la ropa sucia: it seems to be coming from the laundry hamper

Mueven el cesto: they move the hamper

Casi lloran de la emoción: they almost cry out of happiness

Contentas: happy

Encontraron: they found

Tiene mucha hambre: he's very hungry

Se la toma muy rápido: he drinks it very fast

Pequeña camita: little bed

Para que duerma: so that he sleeps

Al día siguiente: the next day

Para ella: for her

Dentro de ella: inside of it

Un collar con cascabel: a collar with a bell

¿Y eso que compraste esto?: how come you bought this?

Ayer: yesterday

Estaban preocupadas por: you were worried about

El estúpido gato: the stupid cat

Me parece que: I think that

Puede ayudar a que lo encuentren: it might help you find him

La próxima vez: next time

Es precioso: it's beautiful

¿Dónde lo compraste?: where did you buy it?

La tienda de mascotas: the pet store

Enfrente de mi oficina: in front of my office

Es un lindo detalle: it's a nice gesture

Están sorprendidas: they are surprised

La actitud de Martina hacia el gato: Martina's attitude towards the cat

Desde ese momento: from that moment

No es tan mala persona: she's not such a bad person

Como ellas pensaban: as they used to think

Ejercicio 1

Contesta las siguientes preguntas – answer the following questions

1- **¿Dónde vive Daniela?** – where does Daniela live?

_____

2- **¿Por qué Daniela no puede vivir sola?** – why can't Daniela live on her own?

_____

3- **¿Cómo es Raquel?** – what is Raquel like?

_____

4- **¿Cómo es Martina?** – what is Martina like?

_____

5- **¿Qué hace el gato todo el día?** – what does the cat do all day?

_____

6- **¿Dónde están los tacones rojos?** – where are the red high heels?

_____

7- **¿De quién son los audífonos blancos?** – who's the owner of the white earphones?

_____

8- **¿Dónde cree Raquel que puede estar el gato?** – where does Raquel think the cat might be?

_____

9- **¿Dónde está el gato?** – where's the cat?

_____

10- **¿Qué compra Martina el día siguiente?** – what does Martina buy the next day?

_____

Ejercicio 2

Elige entre "verdadero" o "falso" – choose "true" or "false"

1- **Daniela vive en un departamento.** – Daniela and Cristina are cousins.

_____

2- **Daniela tiene tres compañeras de piso.** – Daniela has three roommates.

_____

3- **Raquel y Daniela tienen muchas cosas en común.** – Raquel and Daniela have a lot of things in common.

_____

4- **Raquel odia a Martina.** – Raquel hates Martina.

_____

5- **El gato tiene los ojos verdes.** – The cat has green eyes.

_____

6- **El gatito está desaparecido desde anoche.** – The cat's been missing since last night.

_____

7- **Daniela cancela su clase de yoga.** – Daniela cancels her yoga class.

_____

8- **Las chicas casi lloran cuando encuentran al gato.** – The girls almost cry when they find the cat.

_____

9- **Raquel le compra un regalo al gato.** – Raquel buys a gift for the cat.

_____

10- **Daniela cambia de opinión sobre Martina.** – Daniela changes her mind about Martina.

_____

Respuestas – Answers

Ejercicio 1

1- Daniela vive en el barrio de Belgrano, en la ciudad de Buenos Aires.

2- Daniela no puede vivir sola porque necesita a alguien para compartir los gastos del alquiler.

3- Raquel es trabajadora, organizada y servicial.

4- Martina es malhumorada, desconsiderada e incluso maleducada.

5- Lo que el gato hace todo el día es comer, dormir y llorar.

6- Los tacones rojos están debajo de la cama.

7- Los audífonos blancos son de Martina.

8- Raquel cree que el gato puede estar en las cajas vacías en su habitación.

9- El gato está detrás del cesto de ropa sucia en el baño.

10- Martina compra un collar de cascabel para el gato.

Ejercicio 2

1- Falso

2- Falso

3- Verdadero

4- Verdadero

5- Falso

6- Falso

7- Verdadero

8- Verdadero

9- Falso

10- Verdadero

Puntos clave – Key takeaways

- *Mío* and *tuyo* are examples of possessive pronouns.
- Possessive pronouns often substitute the noun that we're referring to. (*Es mío* = it's mine).
- *¿De quién es...?* is a question to ask about possession.
- *Aquí, detrás de, al lado de* are examples of adverbs of place.

In the next chapter, you will learn how to describe someone's appearance in detail and some specific adjectives about personality.

Chapter 8:
La alumna nueva – The new student

Ser valiente es ser libre.
- Séneca

Tomás **estudia cine en una universidad muy conocida** de Bogotá. Aunque **apenas está en el primer semestre, ya ha hecho varios amigos** y a menudo se junta con ellos **a almorzar** o **simplemente a hablar en la cafetería después de clases. Esta tarde** no tienen **mucho que hacer,** así que se juntan en la cafetería a tomar **un café** y comer **un pedazo de torta de vainilla.** Hablan un poco sobre **uno de sus profesores, un**  hombre canoso con las cejas pobladas. También hablan sobre **la alumna nueva,** Camila. Tomás cree que Camila es muy **bonita.** Tiene **unos ojos penetrantes** y **una personalidad** muy misteriosa, **es completamente su tipo de chica. Todos parecen estar de acuerdo con él.**

–**¿Está buena?** –pregunta un amigo de Tomás.

–Sí, tiene **las piernas largas** y **unas caderas anchas** – contesta otro chico.

–**¿De qué color tiene los ojos?**

–**Marrón oscuro.**

–**¿Cómo tiene el pelo? ¿Lo tiene liso?**

–**Tiene el cabello largo y enrulado.**

–A mí me encantan **las chicas con rulos** –dice Tomás.

–**¿Es negra o morena?**

–Es morena y **se nota que tiene la piel suave.**

Luis, **otro amigo de Tomás que estudia odontología, se sienta** en la mesa con ellos y **les pregunta de quién hablan.**

–De la nueva alumna, se llama Camila.

–**¿Cómo es?** –pregunta Luis.

–**¿Físicamente?**

–Sí, físicamente.

Los chicos **buscan una foto de la chica** en Instagram y **se la muestran a Luis.**

–Es hermosa. **Se parece a una actriz famosa.**

–**¿Cuál?**

–**No recuerdo su nombre.**

Tomás ve la foto de la chica y **piensa en las otras cosas que le gustan de ella. Tiene los dientes blancos y derechos, una sonrisa preciosa.** Tiene **varios piercings en las orejas,** y **uno en la nariz, sus mejillas son rosadas.**

–¿**Cómo es como persona?** –pregunta Luis.

–¿**Su personalidad?**

–Sí.

–Pues, está estudiando cine, **eso la hace automáticamente bacana.** Aunque yo creo que **es algo tímida.**

–¿Tímida? Yo creo que **ella es todo lo contrario. Participa en clases** a menudo y **habla con todo el mundo.**

–¿Sí? **Yo la veo muy callada.**

–¿**Estamos hablando de la misma persona?**

–¿**Alguien ya la invitó a salir?** –pregunta Luis.

–**Creo que no** –responde Tomás.

–¿Por qué? ¿**Es intimidante?**

–**Tiene una mirada bastante intimidante.**

–¿**O es que todos ustedes son unos cobardes?**

–**También es una posibilidad.**

–**Yo no la puedo invitar a salir** porque **si mi novia se entera, me mata. ¿Cuál es tu excusa**, Tomás? –pregunta otro amigo.

–Sí, ¿**por qué no la invitas a salir? ¿Tienes novia?**

–No, **no tengo novia** – responde Tomás.

–¿**No quisieras salir con ella?**

–**Obvio** –responde Tomás. –Se nota que **es una persona muy apasionada** y **segura de sí misma. Eso me atrae mucho a ella.**

–Pues **invítala a salir antes de que alguien se te adelante** –dice Luis.

–¿**Y si dice que no?** –pregunta Tomás.

110

–Bueno, **lo aceptas y sigues con tu vida**. Yo sé que tú eres muy indeciso, pero **no pienses tanto las cosas**.

–**¿A dónde debería llevarla?**

–Al cine, **quizás**.

–Sí, es una buena idea.

–Si no la invitas **pronto, la voy a invitar yo** –dice uno de sus amigos.

–**No te creo, a ti te gustan las chicas que son más bajas que tú**, y que tienen **el cabello corto y liso**. También te gustan las chicas **un poco más rellenitas**, ¿no?

–Sí, ese es exactamente mi tipo.

–Lo sé, pero está bien, **mañana la invito a salir, lo prometo. Espero que diga que sí**.

–Sí, **seguro dice que sí. Ella cree que eres gracioso. Capaz hasta piense que eres inteligente**.

–**¿Por qué dices eso?**

–**Ella se río de tus chistes** en clases ayer. **¿Lo recuerdas?**

–Sí, **lo recuerdo. Tienes razón.**

–**Apuesto 1.000 pesos a que dice que no** –dice uno de sus amigos.

–**Ay, sí eres malo**.

El día siguiente, a la hora del almuerzo, Tomás invita a Camila al cine a ver **una película de terror**. En ese momento Camila le dice que no puede salir con él porque tiene novio.

Resumen

Tomás estudia cine en una universidad de Bogotá y un día se junta en la cafetería a hablar con sus amigos. Entre las cosas que hablan, discuten un poco sobre su nueva compañera de clases, una chica llamada Camila. Tomás piensa que ella es muy linda y todos sus amigos parecen pensar lo mismo. Mencionan las cosas que a todos les gusta de ella, tanto físicamente como sobre su personalidad. Al final, los chicos animan a Tomás a que invite a Camila a salir, y Tomás promete que lo hará al día siguiente. Tomás se arma de valor y la invita al cine, pero, por desgracia, Camila le dice que no puede salir con él porque tiene novio.

Summary

Tomás studies film at a university in Bogotá and one day he gets together with his friends in the cafeteria to talk. Among the things they talk about, they bring up their new classmate, a girl called Camila. Tomás thinks she's really pretty and everyone else seems to agree with him. They mention the things they like about her, both physically and personality-wise. In the end, the guys encourage Tomás to ask Camila out, and Tomás promises he will do it the next day. Tomás builds up the courage to ask her out to the movies, but unfortunately, Camila says she can't go out with him because she has a boyfriend.

Glosario – Glossary

Estudia cine: he studies film

En una universidad muy conocida: at a well-known university

Apenas está en el primer semestre: he's just in the first semester

Ya ha hecho varios amigos: he's made some friends

A almorzar: to have lunch

Simplemente a hablar: just to talk

En la cafetería: in the cafeteria

Después de clases: after class

Esta tarde: this afternoon

Mucho que hacer: much to do

Un café: a coffee

Un pedazo de torta de vainilla: a piece of vanilla cake

Uno de sus profesores: one of their professors

Un hombre canoso: a gray-haired man

Con las cejas pobladas: with bushy eyebrows

La alumna nueva: the new student

Bonita: pretty

Unos ojos penetrantes: piercing eyes

Una personalidad muy misteriosa: a very mysterious personality

Es completamente su tipo de chica: she's totally his type of girl

Todos parecen estar de acuerdo con él: they all seem to agree with him

¿Está buena?: is she hot?

Las piernas largas: long legs

Unas caderas anchas: broad hips

¿De qué color tiene los ojos?: what color are her eyes?

Marrón oscuro: dark brown

¿Cómo tiene el cabello?: what's her hair like?

¿Lo tiene liso?: is it straight?

Tiene el cabello largo y enrulado: she has long, curly hair

Las chicas con rulos: girls with curly hair

¿Es negra o morena?: is she black or brunette?

Se nota que tiene la piel suave: you can tell she has soft skin

Otro amigo de Tomás que estudia odontología: another friend of Tomás's who studies dentistry

Les pregunta de quién hablan: he asks them who they're talking about

¿Cómo es?: what is she like? / what does she look like?

¿Físicamente?: physically?

Buscan una foto de la chica: they look for a picture of the girl

Se la muestran a Luis: they show it to Luis

Se parece a una actriz famosa: she looks like a famous actress

¿Cuál?: which one?

No recuerdo su nombre: I don't remember her name

Piensa en las otras cosas que le gustan de ella: he thinks about the other things he likes about her

Tiene los dientes blancos y derechos: she has straight, white teeth

Una sonrisa preciosa: a gorgeous smile

Varios piercings en las orejas: several piercings in her ear

En la nariz: in her nose

Sus mejillas son rosadas: her cheeks are pink

¿Cómo es como persona?: what's she like as a person?

¿Su personalidad?: her personality?

Eso la hace: that makes her

Automáticamente bacana: automatically cool

Es algo tímida: she's a little shy

Es todo lo opuesto: she's the exact opposite

Participa en clases: she participates in class

Habla con todo el mundo: she talks to everyone

Yo la veo muy callada: I think she's pretty quiet

¿Estamos hablando de la misma persona?: are we talking about the same person?

¿Alguien ya la invitó a salir?: did anyone ask her out already?

Creo que no: I don't think so

¿Es intimidante?: is she intimidating?

Tiene una mirada bastante intimidante: her eyes are pretty intimidating

¿O es que todos ustedes son cobardes?: or is it that you're all cowards?

También es una posibilidad: that's another possibility

Yo no la puedo invitar a salir: I can't ask her out

Si mi novia se entera, me mata: if my girlfriend finds out, she will kill me

¿Cuál es tu excusa?: what's your excuse?

¿Por qué no la invitas a salir?: why don't you ask her out?

¿Tienes novia?: do you have a girlfriend?

No tengo novia: I don't have a girlfriend

¿No quisieras salir con ella?: they follow the sound

Obvio: it seems to be coming from the hamper

Es una persona apasionada: she's a very passionate person

Segura de sí misma: confident

Eso me atrae mucho a ella: I really like that about her

Invítala a salir: ask her out (imperative)

Antes de que alguien más se te adelante: before someone else does it before you

¿Y si dice que no?: what if she says no?

Lo aceptas: you accept it

Sigues con tu vida: move on with your life

No pienses tanto las cosas: don't overthink things

¿A dónde debería llevarla?: where should I take her?

Quizás: perhaps

Pronto: soon

La voy a invitar yo: I will ask her out

No te creo: I don't believe you

A ti te gustan las chicas que son: you like girls that are

Más bajas que tú: shorter than you

El cabello corto y liso: short, straight hair

Un poco más rellenitas: a little bit chubbier

Mañana la invito a salir: I will ask her out tomorrow

Lo prometo: I promise

Espero que diga que sí: I hope she says yes

Seguro dice que sí: she will probably say yes

Ella cree que eres gracioso: she thinks you're funny

Capaz hasta piense que eres inteligente: she may even think you're smart

¿Por qué dices eso?: what makes you say that?

Ella se rió de tus chistes: she laughed at your jokes

¿Lo recuerdas?: remember?

Lo recuerdo: I remember

Tienes razón: you're right

Apuesto 1.000 pesos a que dice que no: I bet 1,000 pesos she says no

Ay, sí eres malo: you're so mean

Una película de terror: a horror movie

Ejercicio 1

Contesta las siguientes preguntas – answer the following questions

1- **¿Qué semestre de la carrera estudia Tomás?** – what semester of college is Tomás in?

_____

2- **¿Cómo es su profesor?** – what's his professor like?

_____

3- **¿Cómo es el cabello de Camila?** – what does Camila's hair look like?

_____

4- **¿Qué estudia Luis?** – what's Luis studying?

_____

5- **¿Camila es rubia o morena?** – is Camila blonde or brunette?

_____

6- **¿Qué piensa Tomás de su mirada?** – what does Tomás think about the way she looks at others?

_____

7- **¿Tomás tiene novia?** – does Tomás have a girlfriend?

_____

8- **¿Qué le gusta a Tomás de su personalidad?** – what does Tomás like about her personality?

_____

9- ¿Cómo cree Luis que es Tomás? – what does Luis think of Tomás?

_____

10- ¿Por qué es probable que Camila crea que Tomás es gracioso? – why is it likely Camila thinks Tomás is funny?

_____

Ejercicio 2

Elige entre "verdadero" o "falso" – choose "true" or "false"

1- **Tomás estudia cine.** – Tomás studies film.

_____

2- **Camila tiene los ojos azules.** – Camila has blue eyes.

_____

3- **A Tomás le gustan las chicas con rulos.** – Tomás likes girls with curly hair.

_____

4- **Camila tiene una linda sonrisa.** – Camila has a nice smile.

_____

5- **Camila tiene un piercing en la ceja.** – Camila has a piercing in her eyebrow.

_____

6- **Uno de ellos ya invitó a Camila a salir.** – One of them already asked Camila out.

_____

7- **Tomás no quiere salir con Camila.** – Tomás doesn't want to go out with Camila.

_____

8- **Tomás va a invitar a Camila al cine.** – Tomás is going to ask Camila out to the movies.

_____

9- **Tomás habla con camila en la mañana.** – Tomás talks to Camila in the morning.

10- **Camila rechaza la invitación de Tomás.** – Camila rejects Tomás's invitation.

Respuestas – Answers

Ejercicio 1

1- Tomás está estudiando el primer semestre de la carrera.

2- El profesor de Tomás es un hombre canoso con las cejas pobladas.

3- El cabello de Camila es largo y enrulado.

4- Luis estudia odontología.

5- Camila es morena.

6- Tomás piensa que la mirada de Camila es intimidante.

7- No, Tomás no tiene novia.

8- A Tomás le gusta que Camila sea una persona apasionada y segura de sí misma.

9- Luis cree que Tomás es indeciso.

10- Porque Camila se ríe de los chistes de Tomás.

Ejercicio 2

1- Verdadero

2- Falso

3- Verdadero

4- Verdadero

5- Falso

6- Falso

7- Falso

8- Verdadero

9- Falso

10- Verdadero

Puntos clave – Key takeaways

- *¿Cómo es?* is a question to ask either about someone's appearance or their personality.
- The verb tener is commonly used to describe a person's appearance.
- When we talk about a body part, it is common to use the definite article (*el, la, los, las*) as in *Ella tiene los ojos marrones*.

In the next chapter, you will learn about reflexive verbs, and how to use adverbs of frequency to describe your daily routine.

Chapter 9:
Saliendo a trotar – Going out for a jog

De las dificultades nacen milagros.
- Jean de la Bruyère

Cristina **vive con su novio desde hace un par de meses.** Él **entra muy temprano a su trabajo,** así que **la mayoría del tiempo, él ya no está** cuando ella **se levanta.** Cristina entra a su trabajo a las 9 de la mañana, **lo que le da tiempo de hacer todo con calma. Su alarma suena a las** 7 **y media** y Cristina **se para de la cama** y **se cepilla los dientes. Se prepara una arepa** y la

acompaña con un café con leche. Ve televisión por unos minutos y luego **se prepara para salir a trotar. Ella prefiere trotar a esta hora** porque **no hay tanta gente en la calle. Trota a su ritmo, respirando profundamente** y **apreciando el paisaje. El día es bonito, el cielo está despejado** y **hace sol.** Hay **un parque con muchos árboles**

en **el vecindario de Cristina** que a ella le encanta porque es hermoso y **siempre hay ardillas escalando los árboles**. Ella **a veces alimenta a las ardillas** con fresas o bananas.

Antes de irse del parque, Cristina **se detiene un momento a tomar algo de sol** y a **apreciar los sonidos de la naturaleza. Revisa la hora** en su teléfono y **se apresura de vuelta a casa para no llegar tarde a su trabajo. Aún le falta tomar una ducha** y **vestirse.** Cuando **llega a la puerta de su casa, no consigue las llaves.** No está **en sus bolsillos**, ni en **su riñonera.** Quizás **dejó las llaves** en casa, o **las perdió en el parque**.

Un poco **angustiada**, llama a su novio, pero él **no contesta el teléfono.** Tal vez **está en una reunión** importante, o simplemente **está ocupado.** Cristina **no sabe qué hacer**, ya que no quiere ser **irresponsable** y llegar tarde a su trabajo. **Camina de vuelta al parque, al lugar donde se sentó hace unos minutos** y busca las llaves. Hasta revisa en **un arbusto** pero no ve las llaves **en ningún lado.** Vuelve a la puerta de su casa y **su vecina** le pregunta **si todo está bien, le dice que pase a su casa por una taza de café. El cielo se oscurece** un poco y **hace frío**, así que Cristina **acepta. Es mejor que quedarse esperando en la calle.** Cristina **le envía un correo a su jefe explicando la situación, esperando que él entienda.** Cristina **está molesta consigo misma por ser tan despistada** y **perder las llaves.** Su vecina **le dice que no se preocupe, que esas cosas le pasan a todo el mundo.**

Minutos más tarde, el novio de Cristina al fin contesta el teléfono. Le dice que en este momento está **muy ocupado para salir de la oficina**, pero que en una hora **puede** volver a la casa. Cristina **se resigna** y acepta la situación. **Mientras espera, se pone a jugar con el perro** de la vecina, un perro viejo pero muy **juguetón. Lanza la pelota** y el perro **la busca** y **la trae de vuelta.** Juega con él hasta que su novio llega.

Cristina **corre al baño, se desviste** y se ducha. **Se pone una blusa y una falda** y su novio **le da un aventón** al trabajo. Cristina **se disculpa** con su jefe **por su tardanza** y su jefe le dice que no se preocupe, le dice que **no está molesto con ella** porque ella **siempre llega a la oficina a tiempo. Eso la hace sentir un poco mejor**.

En la noche, **ya sin presión**, Cristina busca sus llaves pero no las encuentra. **Es muy extraño**. Al día siguiente **va al cerrajero** por unas llaves nuevas.

Resumen

Cristina se levanta una mañana, preparada para tener un día normal. Desayuna, ve televisión y sale a trotar un rato al parque cerca de su casa. Cuando vuelve a casa, se da cuenta de que las llaves no están en sus bolsillos. Llama a su novio pero él ya está en el trabajo y no le contesta. Su vecina la invita a esperar en su casa con una taza de café. Se entretiene un rato jugando con el perro de su vecina. Cuando su novio llega, se apresura a ducharse y vestirse para salir al trabajo. Cristina está muy apenada pero su jefe le dice que no se preocupe. Al día siguiente, va al cerrajero por unas llaves nuevas.

Summary

Cristina wakes up one morning, ready to have a normal day. She has breakfast, watches TV, and goes jogging for a while at the park near her house. When she comes back home, she realizes her keys are not in her pockets. She calls her boyfriend, but he's at work so he doesn't pick up the phone. Her neighbor invites her over to her house for a cup of coffee while she waits. She distracts herself playing with her neighbor's dog for a while. When her boyfriend gets home, she rushes to take a shower and get dressed for work. Cristina feels ashamed but her boss tells her not to worry. The next day, she goes to the locksmith for new keys.

Glosario – Glossary

Vive con su novio desde hace un par de meses: she's been living with her boyfriend for a couple of months

Entra muy temprano al trabajo: he starts work pretty early

La mayoría del tiempo: most of the time

Se levanta: she wakes up

Él ya no está: he's already gone

Lo que le da tiempo: which gives her time

De hacer todo con calma: to do everything calmly

Su alarma suena a las 7 y media: her alarm goes off at 7 and half

Se para de la cama: she gets out of bed

Se cepilla los dientes: she brushes her teeth

Se prepara una arepa: she makes herself an arepa

La acompaña con un café con leche: she pairs it with a coffee with milk

Ve televisión por unos minutos: she watches TV for a few minutes

Se prepara para salir a trotar: she gets ready to go jogging

Ella prefiere trotar a esta hora: she prefers to jog at this time

No hay tanta gente en la calle: there aren't that many people on the street

Trota a su ritmo: she jogs at her own pace

Respirando profundamente: breathing deeply

Apreciando el paisaje: taking in the view

El día es bonito: it's a nice day outside

El cielo está despejado: the sky is clear

Hace sol: it's sunny

Un parque con muchos árboles: a park with lots of trees

En el vecindario de Cristina: in Cristina's neighborhood

Siempre hay ardillas: there's always squirrels

Escalando los árboles: climbing the trees

A veces alimenta a las ardillas: she sometimes feeds the squirrels

Se detiene un momento: she stops for a moment

A tomar algo de sol: to take in the sun

Apreciar los sonidos de la naturaleza: to take in the sounds of nature

Revisa la hora: she checks the time

Se apresura de vuelta a casa: she rushes back home

Para no llegar tarde al trabajo: to not be late for work

Aún le falta tomar una ducha: she still has to take a shower

Vestirse: to get dressed

Llega a la puerta de la casa: she gets to her front door

No consigue las llaves: she can't find her keys

En sus bolsillos: in her pockets

Su riñonera: her fanny pack

Dejó las llaves: she left her keys

Las perdió en el parque: she lost them in the park

Angustiada: worried

No contesta el teléfono: he doesn't pick up the phone

Está en una reunión: he's in a meeting

No sabe qué hacer: she doesn't know what to do

Irresponsable: irresponsible

Camina de vuelta al parque: she walks back to the park

Al lugar donde se sentó: to the place where she sat down

Hace unos minutos: a few minutes ago

Un arbusto: a bush

En ningún lado: nowhere

Su vecina: her neighbor (female)

Si todo está bien: if everything is alright

Le dice que pasa a su casa: she invites her into her house

Por una taza de café: for a cup of coffee

El cielo se oscurece: the sky gets dark

Hace frío: it's cold

Acepta: she accepts

Es mejor que: it's better than

Quedarse esperando en la calle: waiting on the street

Le envía un correo a su jefe: she emails her boss

Explicando la situación: explaining the situation

Esperando que él entienda: hoping he will understand

Está molesta consigo misma: she's angry at herself

Por ser tan despistada: for being so absent-minded

Perder las llaves: losing her keys

Le dice que no se preocupe: she tells her not to worry

Que esas cosas le pasan a todo el mundo: that those things happen to everyone

Minutos más tarde: a few minutes later

Muy ocupado para salir de la oficina: too busy to leave the office

Puede: he can

Se resigna: she gives up

Mientras espera: while she waits

Se pone a jugar con el perro: she starts playing with the dog

Juguetón: playful

Lanza la pelota: she throws the ball

La busca: he goes for it

La trae de vuelta: he brings it back

Corre al baño: she runs to the bathroom

Se desviste: she undresses

Se pone una blusa y una falda: she puts on a blouse and a skirt

Le da un aventón: he gives her a ride

Se disculpa: she apologizes

Por su tardanza: for her tardiness

No está molesto con ella: he's not mad at her

Siempre llega a la oficina a tiempo: she always gets to the office on time

Eso la hace sentir mejor: that makes her feel better

Ya sin presión: now without pressure

Es muy extraño: it's very strange

Va al cerrajero: she goes to the locksmith

Ejercicio 1

Contesta las siguientes preguntas – answer the following questions

1- **¿A qué hora se levanta Cristina?** – what time does Cristina wake up?

_____

2- **¿Qué desayuna Cristina?** – what does Cristina have for breakfast?

_____

3- **¿Por qué Cristina prefiere trotar a esa hora?** – why does Cristina prefer to go jogging at that time?

_____

4- **¿Qué animal ve en el parque?** – what animal does she see at the park?

_____

5- **¿Qué hace Cristina antes de irse del parque?** – what does Cristina do before leaving the park?

_____

6- **¿Qué pierde Cristina?** – what does Cristina lose?

_____

7- **¿Por qué Cristina está tan angustiada?** – why is Cristina so worried?

_____

8- **¿Dónde espera Cristina a su novio?** – where does Cristina wait for her boyfriend?

_____

9- **¿Cómo llega Cristina a su trabajo?** – how does Cristina get to work?

_____

10- **¿Por qué el jefe de Cristina no está molesto con ella?** – why is Cristina's boss not mad at her?

_____

Ejercicio 2

Elige entre "verdadero" o "falso" – choose "true" or "false"

1- **Cristina vive con su novio desde hace algunos años.** – Cristina has been living with her boyfriend for a few years.

_____

2- **El novio de Cristina se levanta antes que ella.** – Cristina's boyfriend wakes up before her.

_____

3- **Es una mañana fría.** – It's a cold morning.

_____

4- **El parque queda cerca de su casa.** – The park is near her home.

_____

5- **Cristina a veces alimenta a las ardillas.** – Cristina sometimes feeds the squirrels.

_____

6- **Su vecina le da una taza de café.** – Her neighbor offers her a cup of coffee.

_____

7- **El perro de su vecina la ataca.** – Her neighbor's dog attacks her.

_____

8- **Cristina llama a su jefe para explicarle la situación.** – Cristina calls her boss to explain the situation.

9- **Cristina se pone una blusa y una falda.** – Cristina puts on a blouse and a skirt.

10- **Cristina encuentra las llaves en su cuarto.** – Cristina finds her keys in her room.

Respuestas – Answers

Ejercicio 1

1- Cristina se levanta a las 7 y media.

2- Cristina desayuna una arepa con café con leche.

3- Cristina prefiere trotar a esa hora porque no hay gente en la calle.

4- Cristina ve muchas ardillas en el parque.

5- Antes de irse, Cristina se detiene un momento para tomar sol y apreciar los sonidos de la naturaleza.

6- Cristina pierde sus llaves.

7- Cristina está angustiada porque no quiere llegar tarde a su trabajo.

8- Cristina espera a su novio en la casa de su vecina.

9- El novio de Cristina le da un aventón a su trabajo.

10- El jefe de Cristina no está molesto con ella porque ella siempre llega a tiempo al trabajo.

Ejercicio 2

1- Falso

2- Verdadero

3- Falso

4- Verdadero

5- Verdadero

6- Verdadero

7- Falso

8- Falso

9- Verdadero

10- Falso

Puntos clave – Key takeaways

- Most verbs we use to talk about daily routines are reflexive (*levantarse, cepillarse, bañarse, vestirse*).
- To conjugate a reflexive verb, we put the *se* before the verb and conjugate the verb (*Ella se levanta temprano*).
- *Siempre* and *a veces* are examples of frequency adverbs.
- We can use frequency adverbs to say how often we do things, so it's common to use them when talking about daily routines.

In the next chapter, you will learn more about frequency adverbs and other ways to ask and talk about frequency.

Chapter 10:
El show de comedia –
The comedy show

La experiencia es simplemente el nombre
que le ponemos a nuestros errores.
- Oscar Wilde

Últimamente, Tomás **estudia demasiado**, así que **no ve a sus amigos desde hace más de un mes.** Su amigo Luis **lo invitó a un show de comedia por el centro de Bogotá.** El bar es bonito, con **una decoración playera,** con **colores cálidos** y hasta **un aroma agradable a agua de playa**. Tomás le pide una piña colada al bartender mientras espera a Luis. Tomás **intenta pasarla bien** y **no pensar en todas las cosas que tiene que hacer** para la universidad.

Él **usualmente va al gimnasio al menos dos veces a la semana** y **nunca se pierde su show favorito los viernes en la noche**, pero **en estos días** solo estudia y estudia. **Está exhausto**. Luis lo saluda y le pide un mojito al bartender.

–**¿Estás nervioso?** –pregunta Tomás.

–**Muchísimo**.

–**¿Invitaste a alguien más?**

–**Invité a poca gente. No quiero humillarme frente a todos los que me conocen.**

Hacer standup es algo nuevo para Luis, es solo **un pasatiempo. Es normal que esté así de nervioso**. Tomás le habla de otras cosas **para distraerlo**. Le pregunta sobre **un viejo amigo de ellos**.

–**Casi nunca** veo a Pedro –responde Luis.

–**¿Qué tan seguido ves a Ana?**

–**La veo muy a menudo porque** somos vecinos.

–**Ah, cierto**.

El bar se queda en silencio y **encienden las luces** del pequeño **escenario**. Un chico con **un sombrero les da las gracias a todos por venir** esta noche y **presenta al primer comediante** de la noche. Luis **va a ser** el número cuatro.

Los primeros tres comediantes son **más o menos entretenidos**. No todos sus **chistes** son graciosos y **se nota porque nadie se ríe**. La tercera chica parece ser **la más graciosa**. Es una chica **de lentes** que habla de **su experiencia saliendo con chicos** y ella **recibe muchos aplausos cuando sale del escenario. Llaman el nombre de Luis** y él **se dirige al escenario**. Dice su primer chiste, **algo sobre ser daltónico** y algunas **personas se ríen. Los siguientes** chistes **no son tan graciosos. Nadie se ríe**, e **incluso**

algunos parecen aburridos. Tomás **siente pena por su amigo** pero **le aplaude para animarlo a que continúe.** **Absolutamente** nadie se ríe **con los últimos chistes**, pero al menos le aplauden **cuando se baja del escenario.**

Luis **parece bastante avergonzado. Le dice a Tomás que quiere irse** del bar y él **le dice que está bien.** Van a otro bar **cercano.**

–**Sé honesto. Apesto, ¿verdad?** –pregunta Luis.

–No, **estuvo bien para ser tu primera vez.**

–¿De verdad? **Siento que no tengo talento para esto.**

–Sí, **es normal que no seas perfecto. Con el tiempo aprenderás.**

–No sé, **nadie se reía.**

–Tu primer chiste **fue gracioso** y **la gente se rió.** Quizás puedes hacer más chistes **de ese estilo.**

–Sí, **tengo que practicar más y escribir más.** Esta semana **no practiqué lo suficiente,** pero con la universidad **no tengo tiempo de nada.**

–**Te entiendo, yo estoy igual que tú. No hago las cosas que normalmente disfruto. Por ejemplo,** me gusta ir al cine **todos los sábados. ¿Tú qué tan a menudo haces lo que te gusta,** como **jugar tenis**?

–Normalmente juego tenis los miércoles y viernes, pero sí, **no tengo mucho tiempo** últimamente. Todos los días **tengo que leer algo** o **hacer algo sobre la carrera.**

–Podemos intentar **hacer algo juntos. Nos puede ayudar a sentirnos más motivados.**

–Es una buena idea. ¿Y si vamos mañana domingo a trotar al parque?

–Sí, vamos, **me gustaría**.

–Genial, ahora **a tomar hasta que olvide lo terrible que me fue** esta noche.

Resumen

Luis, el amigo de Tomás, lo invita a un show de comedia en un bar en el centro de Bogotá. Luis va a ser uno de los comediantes que se presente esta noche, así que está muy nervioso ya que es algo nuevo para él. Ellos conversan un rato mientras toman algunos tragos y luego empieza el show. Luis es el cuarto comediante de la noche, y aunque parece empezar bien, el resto de su rutina no parece causarle risa al público. Luis se siente muy avergonzado y le pide a Tomás irse del bar. En otro bar cercano, hablan sobre lo ocupados que están con la universidad últimamente y deciden juntarse para hacer algunas actividades al aire libre.

Summary

Luis, Tomás's friend, invites him to a comedy show in a bar in downtown Bogotá. Luis is going to be one of the comedians in tonight's show, so he's very nervous since this is something new to him. They talk for some time while they have some cocktails, then the show starts. Luis is the fourth comedian of the night, and though he seems to have a good start, the rest of his routine doesn't make the audience laugh. Luis feels really embarrassed and tells Tomás that they should leave the bar. In another bar nearby, they talk about how busy they have been lately with university schoolwork and decide to get together to do some outdoor activities.

Glosario – Glossary

Ultimamente: lately

Estudia demasiado: he studies too much

No ve a sus amigos desde hace más de un mes: he hasn't seen his friends in over a month

Lo invitó a un show de comedia: he invited him to a comedy show

Por el centro de Bogotá: around downtown Bogotá

Una decoración playera: a beach-style decoration

Colores cálidos: warm colors

Un aroma agradable a agua de playa: a pleasant smell of beach water

Intenta pasarla bien: he tries to have a good time

Y no pensar en todas las cosas que tiene que hacer: and not think about all the things he has to do

Usualmente: he usually

Va al gimnasio: goes to the gym

Al menos: at least

Dos veces a la semana: twice a week

Nunca se pierde su show favorito: he never misses his favorite show

Los viernes en la noche: on Friday nights

En estos días: these days

Está exhausto: he's exhausted

¿Estás nervioso?: are you nervous?

Muchísimo: extremely

¿Invitaste a alguien más?: did you invite anyone else?

Invité a poca gente: I invited few people

No quiero humillarme: I don't want to humiliate myself

Frente a todos los que me conocen: in front of everyone I know

Hacer standup es algo nuevo: doing stand-up is something new

Un pasatiempo: a hobby

Es normal que esté así de nervioso: it's normal for him to be this nervous

Para distraerlo: to distract him

Un viejo amigo de ellos: an old friend of theirs

El bar se queda en silencio: everyone in the bar stays silent

Encienden las luces: they turn on the lights

Escenario: stage

Un sombrero: a hat

Les da las gracias a todos por venir: he thanks everyone for coming

Presenta al primer comediante de la noche: he introduces the first comedian of the night

Va a ser: he's going to be

Los primeros: the first ones

Más o menos entretenidos: more or less entertaining

Chistes: jokes

Se nota porque nadie se ríe: you can tell because no one is laughing

La más graciosa: the funniest

De lentes: with glasses

Su experiencia saliendo con chicos: her experience dating guys

Recibe muchos aplausos: she receives lots of applause

Cuando sale del escenario: when she leaves the stage

Llaman el nombre de Luis: they call Luis's name

Se dirije al escenario: he walks to the stage

Algo sobre ser daltónico: something about being color blind

Personas se ríen: people laugh

Los siguientes: the next ones

No son tan graciosos: aren't that funny

Nadie se ríe: no one laughs

Incluso algunos parecen aburridos: some even seem bored

Siente pena por su amigo: he feels sorry for his friend

Le aplaude para animarlo a que continúe: he claps for him to cheer him on to continue

Absolutamente: absolutely

Con los últimos: with the last ones

Cuando se baja del escenario: when he gets off the stage

Parece bastante avergonzado: he seems pretty embarrassed

Le dice a Tomás que quiere irse: he tells Tomás he wants to leave

Le dice que está bien: he says it's fine

Cercano: nearby

Sé honesto: be honest (imperative)

Apesto, ¿verdad?: I suck, right?

Estuvo bien para ser tu primera vez: it was fine for your first time

Siento que no tengo talento para esto: I feel like I don't have the talent for this

Es normal que no seas perfecto: it's normal not to be perfect

Con el tiempo aprenderás: with time you will learn

Nadie se reía: no one was laughing

Fue gracioso: it was funny

La gente se rió: people were laughing

De ese estilo: of that kind

Tengo que practicar más y escribir más: I have to practice more and write more

No practiqué lo suficiente: I didn't practice enough

No tengo tiempo para nada: I don't have time for anything

Te entiendo: I understand you

Yo estoy igual que tú: I'm the same as you

No hago las cosas que normalmente disfruto: I don't do the things I normally enjoy

Por ejemplo: for example

Todos los sábados: every Saturday

¿Qué tan a menudo haces lo que te gusta?: how often do you do what you enjoy?

Jugar tenis: playing tennis

No tengo mucho tiempo: I don't have much time

Tengo que leer algo: I have to read something

Hacer algo para la carrera: to do something for school (university)

Hacer algo juntos: to do something together

Nos puede ayudar a sentirnos motivados: it can helps us feel motivated

Me gustaría: I would like that

A tomar hasta que olvide lo terrible que me fue: let's drink until I forget how terribly I did

Ejercicio 1

Contesta las siguientes preguntas – answer the following questions

1- **¿Cómo es la decoración del bar?** – what's the decoration of the bar like?

_____

2- **¿Qué pide Tomás para tomar?** – what does Tomás order to drink?

_____

3- **¿Qué tan seguido Tomás va al gimnasio?** – how often does Tomás go to the gym?

_____

4- **¿Por qué Luis no invitó a tanta gente al show?** – why didn't Luis invite many people to the show?

_____

5- **¿Cuál es el mejor comediante antes que Luis?** – which is the best comedian before Luis?

_____

6- **¿Sobre qué es el primer chiste de Luis?** – what's Luis's first joke about?

_____

7- **¿Cómo reacciona el público por los chistes de Luis?** – how does the audience react to Luis's jokes?

_____

8- ¿Cómo se siente Luis luego de su turno? – how does Luis feel after his turn?

_____

9- ¿Qué hacen? – what do they do?

_____

10- ¿Qué planean hacer Tomás y Luis? – what do Tomás and Luis plan to do?

_____

Ejercicio 2

Elige entre "verdadero" o "falso" – choose "true" or "false"

1- **Tomás no ve a sus amigos desde hace más de un mes.**
– Luis hasn't seen his friends in over a month.

_____

2- **Tomás casi nunca estudia.** – Tomás almost never studies.

_____

3- **Luis pide una cerveza.** – Luis orders a beer.

_____

4- **Luis siempre hace standup.** – Luis always does stand-up.

_____

5- **Luis ve a su amiga Ana muy a menudo.** – Luis sees his friend Ana very often.

_____

6- **Luis es el quinto comediante de la noche.** – Luis is the fifth comedian of the night.

_____

7- **Nadie aplaude a Luis.** – No one claps for Luis.

_____

8- **Tomás le da ánimos a Luis.** – Tomás gives Luis words of encouragement.

_____

9- **Luis está muy ocupado con la universidad.** – Luis is very busy with schoolwork.

10- **Luis no quiere hacer standup nunca más.** – Luis doesn't want to do stand-up ever again.

Respuestas – Answers

Ejercicio 1

1- La decoración del bar es playera, con colores muy cálidos.

2- Tomás pide una piña colada.

3- Tomás va al gimnasio al menos dos veces a la semana.

4- Porque no quiere humillarse frente a todos los que lo conocen.

5- La mejor comediante antes de Luis es una chica de lentes.

6- El primer chiste de Luis es sobre su experiencia siendo daltónico.

7- El público se ríe del primer chiste de Luis, pero no del resto, varios parecen aburridos.

8- Luis se siente muy avergonzado y hasta cree que no tiene talento para la comedia.

9- Luis y Tomás se van del bar porque Luis se siente muy avergonzado y no quiere estar ahí.

10- Luis y Tomás planean salir a trotar al parque mañana domingo.

Ejercicio 2

1- Verdadero

2- Falso

3- Falso

4- Falso

5- Verdadero

6- Falso

7- Falso

8- Verdadero

9- Verdadero

10- Falso

Puntos clave – Key takeaways

- *¿Qué tan seguido...?* and *¿Qué tan a menudo...?* are questions to ask about frequency.
- *Dos veces a la semana* and *Tres veces al día* are more specific ways to talk about frequency than *siempre* or *a veces*.

In the next chapter, you will learn more vocabulary about the city, other ways to use *haber,* and how to ask about quantity.

Chapter 11:
De visita en Buenos Aires – Visiting Buenos Aires

Un viaje se mide mejor en amigos que en millas.
- Tim Cahill

Sofía viene a Buenos Aires **por primera vez**. Su amiga Daniela vive en la ciudad y **se ofreció a llevarla** a distintos lugares.

Daniela le dice a Sofía que **se puede quedar en su casa**, pero Sofía decide **hospedarse en un hotel**. Ella sabe que Daniela tiene dos compañeras de cuarto y **no quiere ocasionarles ninguna incomodidad**.

Daniela sabe que a Sofía le gusta mucho la historia, así que **planea llevarla** al Cementerio de La Recoleta, **donde algunas personas famosas están enterradas**. En la mañana compran unas medialunas, **que es un tipo de pan dulce** típico en Argentina, y **van a desayunar en** la Plaza del Congreso. El día es **soleado y agradable** y **hay mucha gente a su alrededor desayunando** o **tomando té** y hablando. **Ellas se ponen al día.** Sofía **le cuenta** a Daniela que **pronto se va a mudar a otro país**, quizás Perú, y Daniela le cuenta que también **tiene planes de mudarse. Al principio** piensan en **ir caminando al cementerio**, pero **es mejor idea tomar el metro** de la ciudad en la estación de la Avenida Corrientes que **está a solo tres cuadras. Abordan el metro** y solo hay un **asiento disponible** que **prefieren cederle a una señora mayor.** Siguen conversando pero **están atentas** de **la estación en la que deben bajarse del metro**, la estación Las Heras.

–¿**Cuántas salidas hay?** –pregunta Sofía.

–**Hay varias salidas** en esta estación.

–¿**Por cuál salimos?**

–**Sígueme**.

Salen de la estación y **siguen su camino al cementerio**. En la entrada del cementerio, en las enormes **rejas de metal**, hay **un grupo de extranjeros hablando en inglés**. Les hacen **un par de preguntas** a Daniela y Sofía y ellas responden **tan bien como pueden. Ninguna de las dos habla inglés tan fluido.** El grupo de extranjeros **parece estar esperando a su guía que está un poco atrasado.** Ellas entran al cementerio y **echan un vistazo a su alrededor.** Algunas **capillas** son más modernas que otras, unas **gigantes**, otras pequeñas. Unas parecen **abandonadas**, que **nadie visita en mucho tiempo, lo que a Sofía le parece triste.** Aunque **no hay nadie que la escuche,** Sofía **le pide permiso al espíritu de la persona en la capilla antes de tomar una foto. Junta sus manos como en una oración** y **les da las gracias por permitirle tomar sus fotos.** Ellas **no son las únicas personas** tomando fotos, **especialmente** en **las tumbas de las personas más famosas**, como la tumba de Eva Perón donde hay personas incluso **grabando videos.**

Cuando las chicas **se cansan de caminar** y tomar fotos, van a almorzar unas pizzas en **uno de los lugares favoritos de Daniela**. Sofía le cuenta los planes que tiene, los otros lugares que **quiere visitar** en la ciudad, como **el museo** Malba. Daniela le dice que el museo **no está muy lejos** y que **si quiere la puede llevar**, que ella también **tiene ganas de ver las nuevas exhibiciones** en el museo. Sofía, **encantada**, le dice que sí. **Hablan alrededor de una hora** y toman un autobús hasta Palermo, **donde se encuentra el museo**. Por suerte, **hoy la entrada está a mitad de precio**. A Sofía **le gusta apreciar el arte en silencio** y por un momento **se separa de Daniela**, que **sube al segundo piso** a ver una exhibición distinta. Sofía entra en **una sala enorme** donde exhiben **el trabajo de una fotógrafa chilena** muy **talentosa**. **Las fotos le parecen bellísimas a Sofía** porque **la conmueven** mucho, y su favorita es una **sobre una relación tóxica.**

Al rato, Sofía y Daniela **se encuentran** en una de las salas.

–**¿Cuántas salas hay en este museo?** –pregunta Sofía.

–No sé, creo que un par.

–**¿Hay más de diez?**

–No, **no hay tantas. Hay pocas,** pero son muy grandes.

Sofía y Daniela **recorren todas las salas** del museo y se van. Sofía le agradece a Daniela **por acompañarla**, y **hacen planes de salir otro día** a un bar **a beber.**

Resumen

Sofía, la amiga de Daniela, viene a Buenos Aires por primera vez y Daniela se ofrece a mostrarle la ciudad. Desayunan medialunas en una plaza y luego visitan el Cementerio de La Recoleta, donde algunas personas famosas están enterradas. Sofía tiene la oportunidad de tomar muchas fotos y aprender sobre el lugar. La última parada es un museo llamado Malba en Palermo, donde Sofía aprecia unas hermosas fotografías de una talentosa fotógrafa. Al final del día, las chicas hacen planes para verse otro día.

Summary

Sofía, Daniela's friend, comes to Buenos Aires for the very first time and Daniela offers to show her the city. They have *medialunas* for breakfast in a square and then they visit the Recoleta Cemetery, where several famous people are buried. Sofía has the opportunity to take loads of pictures and learn about the place. The last stop is a museum called Malba in Palermo, where Sofía sees some beautiful pictures from a talented photographer. At the end of the day, the girls make plans to see each other another day.

Glosario – Glossary

Por primera vez: for the first time

Se ofreció a llevarla: she offered to take her

Se puede quedar en su casa: she can stay at her place

Hospedarse en un hotel: to stay in a hotel

No quiere causarles ninguna incomodidad: she doesn't want to inconvenience them

Planea llevarla a: she plans to take her

Donde algunas personas famosas están enterrada: where some famous people are buried

Que es un tipo de pan dulce: which is a type of pastry

Típico en Argentina: common in Argentina

Van a desayunar en: they go have breakfast in

Soleado y agradable: sunny and nice

Hay mucha gente: there are a lot of people

A su alrededor: around them

Desayunando: having breakfast

Tomando té: drinking tea

Ellas se ponen al día: they catch up

Le cuenta: she tells her

Pronto se va a mudar a otro país: she's going to move to another country soon

Tiene planes de mudarse: she has plans of moving out

Al principio: at the beginning

Ir caminando al cementerio: to walk to the cemetery

Es mejor idea tomar el metro: it's a better idea to take the subway

Está a solo tres cuadras: it's just three blocks away

Abordan el metro: they board the subway

Asiento disponible: seat available

Prefieren cederle a una señora mayor: they prefer to give it up to an older woman

Están atentas: they are alert

La estación en la que deben bajarse del metro: the station in which they have to get off the subway

¿Cuántas salidas hay?: how many exits are there?

Hay varias salidas: there are several exits

¿Por cuál salimos?: which one should we take?

Sígueme: follow me

Siguen su camino al cementerio: they continue their way to the cemetery

Rejas de metal: metal bars

Un grupo de extranjeros: a group of foreigners

Hablando en inglés: speaking English

Un par de preguntas: a couple of questions

Tan bien como pueden: as well as they can

Ninguna de las dos: neither of them

Habla inglés tan fluido: speak English as fluently

Parece estar esperando a su guía: they seem to be waiting for their tour guide

Que está un poco atrasado: who is a little late

Echan un vistazo a su alrededor: they take a look around

Capillas: chapels

Gigantes: huge

Abandonadas: abandoned

Nadie visita en mucho tiempo: no one has visited in a long time

Lo que a Sofía le parece triste: which Sofía finds sad

No hay nadie que la escuche: there's no one who can hear her

Le pide permiso al espíritu de la persona en la capilla: she asks for permission to the spirit of the person in the chapel

Antes de tomar una foto: before taking a picture

Junta sus manos como en una oración: she puts her hands together as if in prayer

Les da las gracias: she thanks them

Por permitirle tomar sus fotos: for letting her take her pictures

No son las únicas personas: they're not the only people

Especialmente: especially

Las tumbas de las personas más famosas: the graves of the most famous people

Grabando videos: recording videos

Se cansan de caminar: they get tired of walking

Uno de los lugares favoritos de Daniela: one of Daniela's favorite places

Quiere visitar: she wants to visit

El museo: the museum

No está muy lejos: it's not very far

Si quiere la puede llevar: she can take her there if she wants to

Tiene ganas de ver las nuevas exhibiciones: she wants to see the new exhibitions

Encantada: more than happy

Hablan alrededor de una hora: they talk for about an hour

Donde se encuentra el museo: where the museum is at

Hoy la entrada está a mitad de precio: the ticket is half price today

Le gusta apreciar el arte en silencio: she likes to appreciate art in silence

Se separa de Daniela: she and Daniela split

Sube al segundo piso: she goes up to the second floor

Una sala enorme: a huge room

El trabajo de una fotógrafa chilena: the work of a Chilean photographer

Talentosa: talented

Las fotos le parecen bellísimas a Sofía: Sofía thinks the pictures are really beautiful

La conmueven: they move her

Sobre una relación tóxica: about a toxic relationship

Al rato: later

Se encuentran: they meet

¿Cuántas salas hay en este museo?: how many rooms are there in this museum?

161

¿Hay más de diez?: are there more than ten?

No hay tantas: there aren't that many

Hay pocas: there are a few

Recorren todas las salas: they go through all the rooms

Por acompañarla: for coming with her

Hacen planes de salir otro día: they make plans to go out another day

A beber: to drink

Ejercicio 1

Contesta las siguientes preguntas – answer the following questions

1- **¿Por qué Sofía no se queda con Daniela?** – why isn't Sofía staying with Daniela?

_____

2- **¿Qué desayunan?** – what do they have for breakfast?

_____

3- **¿Qué le cuenta Sofía a Daniela?** – what does Sofía tell Daniela?

_____

4- **¿Cómo van al cementerio?** – how do they go to the cemetery?

_____

5- **¿En qué estación se bajan?** – at what station do they get off?

_____

6- **¿A quién se encuentran en la entrada del cementerio?** – who do they meet at the entrance of the cemetery?

_____

7- **¿Qué hace Sofía antes de tomar fotos en las capillas?** – what does Sofía do before taking pictures in the chapels?

_____

8- **¿Las entradas del museo son costosas?** – are the tickets to the museum expensive?

_____

9- **¿Por qué a Sofía le encantan tanto las fotos en el museo?** – why does Sofía like the pictures in the museum so much?

_____

10- **¿Qué planean hacer otro día?** – what do they plan to do another day?

_____

Ejercicio 2

Elige entre "verdadero" o "falso" – choose "true" or "false"

1- Sofía se hospeda en un hotel. – Sofía is staying in a hotel.

_____

2- Ellas desayunan en una cafetería. – They have breakfast at a coffee shop.

_____

3- Ellas van al cementerio en autobús. – They go to the cemetery by bus.

_____

4- Ellas le ceden su puesto a una señora mayor. – They give up their seat to an older lady.

_____

5- Los extranjeros hablan francés. – The foreigners speak French.

_____

6- Todas las capillas son muy similares. – All the chapels are very similar.

_____

7- El museo queda en Palermo. – The museum is in Palermo.

_____

8- La fotógrafa es argentina. – The photographer is Argentinian.

_____

9- **Hay pocas salas en el museo.** – There are just a few rooms in the museum.

___

10- **Ellas hacen planes de ir a cenar.** – They make plans to go out for dinner.

___

Respuestas – Answers

Ejercicio 1

1- Sofía no se queda con Daniela porque sabe que ella tiene dos compañeras de cuarto y no quiere causarles incomodidades.

2- Sofía y Daniela desayunan medialunas.

3- Sofía le cuenta a Daniela que piensa mudarse a otro país, quizás Perú.

4- Sofía y Daniela van al cementerio en el metro de la ciudad.

5- Sofía y Daniela se bajan en la estación Las Heras.

6- Sofía y Daniela se encuentran a unos extranjeros en la entrada del cementerio.

7- Sofía les pide permiso a los espíritus en las capillas antes de tomar una foto.

8- No, las entradas del museo están a mitad de precio hoy.

9- A Sofía le encantan las fotos en el museo porque la conmueven mucho.

10- Sofía y Daniela planean salir a un bar a beber otro día.

Ejercicio 2

1- Verdadero

2- Falso

3- Falso

4- Verdadero

5- Falso

6- Falso

7- Verdadero

8- Falso

9- Verdadero

10- Falso

Puntos clave – Key takeaways

- *¿Cuántos...?* and *¿Cuántas...?* are used with countable nouns.
- *¿Cuánto...?* and *¿Cuánta...?* are used with uncountable nouns.
- *Tantas* and *pocas* are examples of quantifiers, which we can use to give an approximate amount of something.

In the next chapter, you will learn how to ask and talk about the weather in detail.

Chapter 12:
A la playa – Going to the beach

Un buen viajante no tiene planes.
- Confucio

Tomás y sus amigos **van a ir a la playa** este viernes **aprove-chando que es un fin de semana largo**. Todos se levantan muy temprano la mañana del viernes y **se encuentran en la terminal de autobuses** donde un autobús enorme **los espera para llevarlos** a la playa. Luis, el amigo de Tomás, **alquiló el autobús por el día, lo que es un poco caro** pero **es posible pagarlo entre todos**. El autobús **arranca** a las 6 de la mañana **para evitar el tráfico** y **llegar a la playa antes de las 8. Entre Tomás y sus amigos, hay alrededor de dieciséis personas** en el autobús. Algunos son **compa-ñeros de clases**, otros **amigos que estudian otras carreras**. Algunos **toman una siesta** antes de llegar a la playa, otros

empiezan a tomar cervezas o comer alguna chuchería. El viaje a la playa es tranquilo, no hay mucho tráfico y el cielo está despejado. Es un día perfecto para ir a la playa.

El autobús los deja cerca de un local donde venden sándwiches y empanadas. Los chicos desayunan y luego van al puerto donde se montan en unas lanchas para ir a la isla donde queda la playa. Algunos no quieren montarse en las lanchas porque les da miedo caerse al agua, pero es la única forma de llegar a la isla. Las olas sacuden el bote y unas chicas gritan mientras que otros se ríen o sacan fotos y videos. Todos llegan bien a la isla, aunque Tomás se siente un poco mareado. Piensa que desayunar y montarse en la lancha no fue una buena idea.

Son aproximadamente las 8 de la mañana y la playa comienza a llenarse de gente. Los chicos dejan sus cosas en un lugar que reservaron donde hay sillas playeras y paraguas muy grandes para cuidarlos del sol. Todos se desvisten, quedándose en shorts o trajes de baño, se ayudan a colocarse protector solar para no quemarse, y luego corren al agua. La playa es hermosa, con arena marrón clara y el agua es cristalina, parece agua de pecera. La gente juega en el agua, con las olas, se toman fotos, juegan con pelotas playeras, y hasta juegan excavando hoyos en la arena.

Un par de horas más tarde, el cielo se nubla un poco. Hace algo de frío. Los chicos salen del agua y vuelven al lugar donde están sus cosas. Hace viento y a los minutos comienza a llover.

—¿Cuántos grados hace? —pregunta uno de los chicos.

—Hace 19 grados —responde Tomás.

—¿Va a llover todo el día? Yo veo relámpagos.

—No, yo creo que es temporal. Tenemos que esperar.

—Pero **es raro, en un momento hace buen tiempo** y **el cielo está claro**, y **luego el cielo se oscurece de repente**, y no es temporada de lluvia. **¿Y si hay neblina o comienza a caer granizo?**

—**Estás exagerando, eso no va a pasar.**

Los chicos hablan, beben y **juegan cartas para pasar el rato. Tienen la esperanza de que el tiempo mejore** ya que en la tarde **tienen que volver al autobús que los llevará a casa.** Luis siempre **pierde jugando este tipo de juegos de beber** y **termina borracho primero que los demás.** Se ríe mucho y **dice cosas graciosas.** Quiere ir al agua **a pesar de la lluvia** y los demás **no lo dejan** porque **les parece peligroso.**

—**¿Estás loco? ¿Y si te ahogas?** —dice Tomás.

Todos siguen jugando y **pasándola bien.** A eso de las 2 de la tarde **deja de llover** y **sale el sol.** Los chicos almuerzan **pescado frito** y **esperan a que haga más sol** para ir al agua. Luis **se queda dormido** en una silla **mientras los demás se divierten** en el agua. **Lo despiertan cuando es hora de irse.** Luis **siente un poco de pena por embriagarse** pero cuando se montan en el autobús **ya no es el único ebrio.** Todos siguen tomando y escuchando música **todo el camino de vuelta. El conductor del autobús hace una parada** en una **gasolinera** porque algunos chicos **tienen ganas de vomitar. Les toma un par de horas** llegar a casa porque hay mucho tráfico ya que a esta hora **todos vuelven a casa de la playa. A pesar de todo**, los chicos se divierten mucho y le agradecen a Luis por **organizar la salida** y alquilar el autobús.

Resumen

Tomás y sus amigos se van a la playa en un autobús el viernes en la mañana. El autobús los deja en un puerto donde deben tomar unas lanchas para llegar a la isla. Disfrutan del sol y el agua durante un par de horas hasta que el cielo se oscurece y comienza a llover. Los chicos toman cervezas y juegan cartas para pasar el tiempo. Luis toma mucho y se emborracha. Cuando el cielo se despeja, él se queda dormido en una de las sillas mientras los demás se divierten. En la tarde vuelven al autobús. Varios chicos toman demasiado y tienen que hacer una parada en una gasolinera para que ellos puedan vomitar. A pesar de todo eso, Tomás y sus amigos la pasan muy bien.

Summary

Tomás and his friends go to the beach on a bus on Friday morning. The bus drops them off at the port, where they have to take some boats to get to the island. They enjoy the sun and the water for a couple of hours until the sky goes dark and it starts raining. The guys have some beers and play cards to kill time. Luis drinks a lot and gets drunk. When it stops raining, he falls asleep in one of the chairs while the rest have fun. They get back on the bus in the afternoon. Some of them drink too much and they have to make a stop at a gas station so that they can throw up. In spite of it all, Tomás and his friends have a really good time.

Glosario – Glossary

Van a ir a la playa: they're going to go to the beach

Aprovechando que es un fin de semana largo: taking advantage of the fact that it is a long weekend

Se encuentran en la terminal de autobuses: they meet at the bus terminal

Los espera para llevarlos: it waits for them to take them there

Alquiló el autobús por el día: he rented the bus for the day

Lo que es un poco caro: which is a little expensive

Es posible pagarlo entre todos: it's possible to pay for it together

Arranca: it takes off

Evitar el tráfico: to avoid traffic

Llegar a la playa antes de las 8: to arrive at the beach before 8

Entre Tomás y sus amigos: between Tomás and his friends

Hay alrededor de dieciséis personas: there are around sixteen people

Compañeros de clases: classmates

Amigos que estudian otras carreras: friends that study other majors

Toman una siesta: they take a nap

Empiezan a tomar: they start drinking

Comer chucherías: to eat snacks

Es tranquilo: it's quiet

No hay mucho tráfico: there isn't much traffic

El cielo está despejado: the sky is clear

Es un día perfecto: it's a perfect day

Los deja cerca de un local donde venden sándwiches y empanadas: it drops them off near a place where they sell sandwiches and empanadas

El puerto: the port

Se montan en unas lanchas: they get on some boats

La isla donde queda la playa: the island where the beach is located

No quieren montarse en las lanchas: they don't want to get on the boats

Les da miedo caerse al agua: they're afraid of falling into the water

Es la única forma de llegar a la isla: it's the only way to get to the island

Las olas sacuden el bote: the waves rock the boat

Unas chicas gritan: some girls scream

Mientras otros se ríen: while others laugh

Todos llegan bien a la isla: they all make it to the island just fine

Se siente un poco mareado: he feels a little dizzy

No fue una buena idea: it wasn't a good idea

Comienza a llenarse de gente: it starts to fill up with people

Dejan sus cosas en un lugar que reservaron: they leave their things in a place they reserved

Sillas playeras: beach chairs

Paraguas: umbrellas

Para cuidarlos del sol: to shield them from the sun

Se desvisten: they undress

Trajes de baño: bathing suits

Se ayudan a colocarse protector solar: they help each other put on sunscreen

Para no quemarse: to not get sunburned

Arena marrón clara: light-brown sand

El agua es cristalina: the water is crystal clear

Pecera: fish tank

Pelotas playeras: beach balls

Escavando hoyos en la arena: digging holes in the sand

Un par de horas más tarde: a couple of hours later

El cielo se nubla: it gets cloudy

Hace un poco de frío: it's a little cold

Hace viento: it's windy

Comienza a llover: it starts raining

¿Cuántos grados hace?: what's the temperature?

Hace 19 grados: it's 19 degrees

¿Va a llover todo el día?: is it going to rain all day?

Yo veo relámpagos: I see lightning

Es temporal: it's temporary

Tenemos que esperar: we have to wait

Es raro: it's strange

En un momento hace buen tiempo: one moment the weather's fine

El cielo está claro: the sky is clear

Luego el cielo se oscurece de repente: then the sky gets dark all of a sudden

No es temporada de lluvia: it's not rainy season

¿Y si hay neblina o comienza a caer granizo?: what if there's mist or it starts to hail?

Estás exagerando: you're overreacting

Eso no va a pasar: that's not going to happen

Juegan cartas para pasar el rato: they play with cards to pass the time

Tienen la esperanza de que el tiempo mejore: they have hopes that the weather will improve

Tienen que volver al autobús que los llevará a casa: they have to get back on the bus that will take them home

Pierde jugando este tipo de juegos de beber: he loses playing these kinds of drinking games

Termina borracho primero que los demás: he ends up drunk before anyone else

Dice cosas graciosas: he says funny things

A pesar de la lluvia: despite the rain

No lo dejan: they don't let him

Les parece peligroso: they think it's dangerous

¿Estás loco?: are you insane?

¿Y si te ahogas?: what if you drown?

Pasándola bien: having a good time

Deja de llover: it stops raining

Sale el sol: the sun comes out

Pescado frito: fried fish

Esperan a que haga más sol: they wait for it to be sunnier

Se queda dormido: he falls asleep

Mientras los demás se divierten: while the rest have fun

Lo despiertan cuando es hora de irse: they wake him up when it's time to leave

Siente pena por embriagarse: he feels embarrassed for getting drunk

Ya no es el único ebrio: he's not the only one drunk anymore

Todo el camino de vuelta: all the way back

El conductor del autobús hace una parada: the bus driver makes a stop

Gasolinera: gas station

Tienen ganas de vomitar: they feel like throwing up

Les toma un par de horas: it takes them a couple of hours

Todos vuelven a casa: they're all going back home

A pesar de todo: in spite of everything

Organizar la salida: organizing the trip

Ejercicio 1

Contesta las siguientes preguntas – answer the following questions

1- ¿Por qué van a la playa un viernes en la mañana? – why are they going to the beach on a Friday morning?

_____

2- ¿A qué hora arranca el autobús? – what time does the bus leave?

_____

3- ¿Cuántas personas hay en el autobús? – how many people are there in the bus?

_____

4- ¿Por qué a algunos les da miedo montarse en las lanchas? – why are some of them afraid of getting on the boat?

_____

5- ¿Cómo es la playa? – what's the beach like?

_____

6- ¿Qué hace la gente alrededor? – what do the people around them do?

_____

7- ¿Por qué los chicos salen del agua? – why do the guys get out of the water?

_____

8- ¿Por qué Luis termina borracho primero? – why does Luis end up drunk first?

9- ¿A qué hora vuelven a entrar al agua? – what time do they get back in the water?

10- ¿Por qué se detienen en una gasolinera? – why do they stop at a gas station?

Ejercicio 2

Elige entre "verdadero" o "falso" – choose "true" or "false"

1- Los chicos se encuentran en casa de Tomás para salir a la playa. – They guys meet at Tomás's house to leave for the beach.

2- Tomás alquila un autobús para que los lleve a la playa. – Tomás rents a bus to take them to the beach.

3- Tomás se marea en la lancha. – Tomás gets seasick on the boat.

4- No hay casi gente en la playa. – There aren't that many people on the beach.

5- Los chicos se meten al agua a pesar de la lluvia. – The guys get in the water despite the rain.

6- Todos almuerzan pescado frito. – Everyone has fried fish for lunch.

7- Luis se queda dormido en una silla. – Luis falls asleep on a chair.

8- **Luis vomita en el autobús.** – Luis throws up on the bus.

9- **Hay mucho tráfico en el camino de vuelta a casa.** – There's a lot of traffic on the way back home.

10- **Todos le agradecen a Luis por organizar todo.** – They all say thank you to Luis for organizing everything.

Respuestas – Answers

Ejercicio 1

1- Van a la playa un viernes en la mañana porque aprovechan que es un fin de semana largo.

2- El autobús arranca a las 6 de la mañana.

3- Hay alrededor de 16 personas en el autobús.

4- A algunos les da miedo montarse en las lanchas porque no quieren caer al agua.

5- La playa es hermosa, con arena marrón clara y agua cristalina.

6- La gente alrededor juega en el agua, se toman fotos, juegan con pelotas playeras y hasta excavan huecos en la arena.

7- Los chicos salen del agua porque comienza a hacer frío y a llover.

8- Luis termina borracho primero porque siempre pierde jugando juegos de beber.

9- Los chicos vuelven a entrar al agua a eso de las 2 de la tarde que el clima mejora.

10- Se detienen en una gasolinera porque algunos de los chicos tienen ganas de vomitar.

Ejercicio 2

1- Falso

2- Falso

3- Verdadero

4- Falso

5- Falso

6- Verdadero

7- Verdadero

8- Falso

9- Verdadero

10- Verdadero

Puntos clave – Key takeaways

- The verb *hacer* is used impersonally to talk about weather (*Hace frío* = it's cold).
- *¿Cómo está el clima?* is how you ask about the weather.
- *¿Cómo está la temperatura?*, *¿Cuántos grados hace?* and *¿A cuántos grados estamos?* are ways to ask about the temperature.
- *Hace 20 grados* and *estamos a 20 grados* are ways to answer those questions.

In the next chapter, you will learn vocabulary about the hair, how to use reciprocal pronouns, and other reflexive verbs.

Chapter 13:
Un nuevo look – A new look

*Por sobre la oreja fina baja lujoso el cabello, lo mismo
que una cortina que se levanta hacia el cuello.*
- José Martí

Marisol y su hermana **tienen cita hoy en la peluquería** Las Cuatro Rosas **para cortarse el cabello.** Marisol **está un poco aburrida de su cabello** y **quiere probar algo nuevo pero aún no sabe qué.** Ella **espera que en la peluquería se le ocurra algo.** Marisol y su hermana llegan a la peluquería a las 3 de la tarde, justo a tiempo para sus citas, pero **sus peluqueras de confianza** están ocupadas así que **tienen que esperar un rato.** Se sientan en las sillas a esperar. Marisol **le da una ojeada a las revistas de chismes** pero son muy viejas, **de hace más de quince años**, así que prefiere hablar con su hermana.

–¿Qué te pasó en la mano? –pregunta Marisol.

–**No es nada. Me quemé** –responde su hermana.

–**¿No te duele?**

–**No, ya no.**

–**Eres muy descuidada.**

–**Mira quién habla. Tú te cortas todo el tiempo** cuando cocinas.

–Sí, tienes razón.

–Y **cada tanto te caes caminando en la calle.**

–Sí, ya, **yo soy descuidada como tú.**

La peluquera de Marisol **se desocupa** y la lleva al **lavabo de cabello** para **aplicarle champú**. El agua es **tibia** y agradable. La chica **le masajea el cabello** con **movimientos circulares** y Marisol se siente muy relajada. El champú **huele a coco** y a Marisol le encanta, le pregunta a la chica el nombre del champú **para comprarlo**. Después del lavado, la chica **envuelve el cabello de Marisol en una toalla** y la lleva a **su estación para proceder a cortarle el cabello**.

–**¿Qué te quieres hacer en el pelo?** –pregunta la chica.

–**La verdad**, no sé. Quiero algo diferente.

–¿Quieres **un peinado diferente** o quieres **otro color**?

–**Quiero que me cortes las puntas** y quiero otro color. Ya **estoy aburrida del rubio.**

–**¿Qué te parece en negro?**

–No lo sé.

La chica **le da un catálogo con varios colores** a Marisol **para que se decida qué color quiere,** o si prefiere **el mismo** color. **Mientras tanto,** comienza a **cortarle las**

puntas con **una tijera profesional**. La hermana de Marisol se sienta en la silla de al lado y **le da su opinión sobre qué color sería mejor**.

–¿**Sabes qué? Escoge tú un color** –dice Marisol.

–¿**Segura?** –responde la peluquera.

–Sí, **sorpréndeme.**

Marisol **se ve en el espejo** una vez más y, **en su mente, se despide del rubio** en su cabello.

–Yo a veces **me corto el cabello yo misma** –dice la hermana de Marisol.

–¿**Tú misma? ¿Por qué haces eso?** –dice Marisol.

–**Lo hago** cuando tengo las puntas muy **dañadas, secas**, y **no tengo tiempo** para ir a la peluquería.

–**Qué locura.**

–Antes **nos cortábamos el cabello la una a la otra. ¿No te acuerdas?**

–**Eso fue hace muchos años.**

–**Tú tenías otra peluquera antes**, ¿no? ¿**Qué pasó?**

–**No nos vemos desde que se mudó a Madrid.**

–**Ay, qué mal.** Pero tu nueva peluquera es **excelente.**

–**Así es.**

La chica **le aplica el colorante** a Marisol, luego **le seca el cabello. Cuando está listo**, le dice a Marisol que se mire en el espejo. Su cabello es **rojo** ahora.

–¿**Te gusta?** –pregunta la peluquera.

–Me encanta. **Me gusta como me veo pelirroja.**

–¿**Quieres que te haga las uñas también?**

–Sí, **yo no sé pintarme las uñas.**

–**¿Qué pintura quieres?**

–**Rosado,** o quizás rojo **para que combine con el cabello.**

Marisol y su hermana salen de la peluquería **luego de cuatro horas.**

–**¿En serio te gustó?** –pregunta la hermana de Marisol.

–No, **lo odio, me quedó horrible.**

–**¿Por qué no dijiste nada?**

–No sé, **entré en pánico. ¿Se ve muy mal?**

–**Al menos a mí me gusta mi nuevo corte.**

Marisol **se arrepiente de pintarse el cabello.** Ahora **extraña** su color rubio.

Resumen

Marisol y su hermana tienen una cita en la peluquería Las Cuatro Rosas a las 3 de la tarde. Marisol está cansada de tener el cabello rubio, pero no está segura de qué se quiere hacer. Ella espera que en la peluquería se le ocurra algo. Marisol espera un rato a que su peluquera esté desocupada, luego ella le lava el cabello y le corta las puntas. Marisol sigue indecisa sobre el color, así que lo deja en las manos de su peluquera. Marisol le dice a su peluquera que le encantó el nuevo color, pero al salir de la peluquería le dice a su hermana la verdad: odia su nuevo color y se arrepiente de pintarse el cabello de rojo.

Summary

Marisol and her sister have an appointment at the salon *Las Cuatro Rosas* at 3 in the afternoon. Marisol is tired of having blonde hair but she's not sure what she wants. She hopes that she will come up with something at the salon. Marisol waits for her hair stylist to be available, then she washes Marisol's hair and trims her ends. Marisol is still unsure about the color, so she leaves it in her stylist's hands. Marisol tells her stylis that she liked the new color, but when they leave the salon, she tells her sister the truth: she hates the new color and she regrets dying her hair red.

Glosario – Glossary

Tienen una cita hoy en la peluquería: they have an appointment at the hair salón today

Para cortarse el cabello: to get a haircut

Está un poco aburrida de su cabello: she's a little bored of her hair

Quiere probar algo nuevo: she wants to try something new

Pero aún no sabe qué: but she doesn't know what yet

Espera que en la peluquería se le ocurra algo: she hopes she will come up with something at the salon

Sus peluqueras de confianza: the hair stylist they like

Tienen que esperar un rato: they have to wait for a while

Le da una ojeada a: she takes a look at

Las revistas de chismes: the gossip magazines

De hace más de quince años: from more than fifteen years ago

¿Qué te pasó en la mano?: what happened to your hand?

No es nada: it's nothing

Me quemé: I burned myself

¿No te duele?: doesn't it hurt?

Ya no: not anymore

Eres muy descuidada: you're so clumsy

Mira quién habla: look who's talking

Tú te cortas todo el tiempo: you cut yourself all the time

Cada tanto: every now and then

Te caes caminando en la calle: you fall on the street while walking

Yo soy descuidada como tú: I'm clumsy like you

Se desocupa: she is available

Lavabo de cabello: hair basin

Aplicarle champú: to apply shampoo on her hair

Tibia: lukewarm

Le masajea el cabello: she massages her hair

Movimientos circulares: circular movements

Huele a coco: it smells like coconut

Para comprarlo: to buy it

Envuelve el cabello de Marisol en una toalla: she wraps Marisol's hair in a towel

Su estación: her station

Para proceder a cortarle el cabello: to proceed to cut her hair

¿Qué te quieres hacer en el pelo?: what do you want for your hair?

La verdad: honestly

Un peinado diferente: a different hair style

Otro color: another color

Quiero que me cortes las puntas: I want you to trim my ends

Estoy aborrida del rubio: I'm bored of the blonde hair

¿Qué te parece negro?: what do you think about black?

Le da un catálogo de varios colores: she gives her a catalog with several colors

Para que se decida qué color quiere: so she can decide what color she wants

El mismo: the same

Mientras tanto: meanwhile

Cortarle las puntas: to trim her ends

Una tijera profesional: professional scissors

Le da su opinión sobre qué color sería mejor: she tells her which color she thinks will be best

¿Sabes qué?: you know what?

Escoge tú: you choose

¿Segura?: are you sure?

Sorpréndeme: surprise me

Se ve en el espejo: she looks at herself in the mirror

En su mente: in her mind

Se despide del rubio: she says goodbye to the blonde

Me corto el cabello yo misma: I cut my own hair

¿Tú misma?: on your own?

¿Por qué haces eso?: why do you do that?

Lo hago: I do it

Dañadas: damaged

Secas: dry

No tengo tiempo: I don't have time

Qué locura: that's insane

Nos cortábamos el cabello la una a la otra: we used to cut each other's hair

¿No te acuerdas?: don't you remember?

Eso fue hace muchos años: that was many years ago

Tú tenías otra peluquera antes: you used to have another hair stylist

¿Qué pasó?: what happened?

No nos vemos desde que se mudó a Madrid: we haven't seen each other since she moved to Madrid

Ay, qué mal: that's too bad

Excelente: excellent

Así es: that's right

Le aplica el colorante: she applies the hair dye

Le seca el cabello: she blow-dries her hair

Cuando está listo: when it's done

Rojo: red

¿Te gusta?: do you like it?

Me gusta como me veo pelirroja: I like how I look as a readhead

¿Quieres que te haga las uñas también?: do you want me to do your nails too?

Yo no sé pintarme las uñas: I don't know how to do my nails

¿Qué pintura quieres?: what nail polish do you want?

Rosado: pink

Para que combine con el cabello: so it matches my hair

Luego de cuatro horas: after four hours

¿En serio te gustó?: did you really like it?

Lo odio: I hate it

Me quedó horrible: it looks horrible

¿Por qué no dijiste nada?: why didn't you say anything?

Entré en pánico: I panicked

¿Se ve muy mal?: does it look that bad?

Al menos: at least

A mí me gusta mi corte: I like my new haircut

Se arrepiente de pintarse el cabello: she regrets dying her hair

Extraña: she misses

Ejercicio 1

Contesta las siguientes preguntas – answer the following questions

1- **¿Por qué Marisol quiere un nuevo look?** – why does Marisol want a new look?

_____

2- **¿A qué hora es la cita de Marisol en la peluquería?** – what time is Marisol's appointment at the hair salon?

_____

3- **¿Qué tan viejas son las revistas?** – how old are the magazines?

_____

4- **¿Por qué Marisol es descuidada?** – why is Marisol clumsy?

_____

5- **¿A qué huele el champú?** – what does the shampoo smell like?

_____

6- **¿Qué quiere Marisol que le hagan?** – what does Marisol want to get done?

_____

7- **¿Por qué la hermana de Marisol se corta el cabello ella misma?** – why does Marisol's sister cut her own hair?

_____

8- ¿Qué pasó con la peluquera anterior de Marisol? – what happened to Marisol's previous hair stylist?

_____

9- ¿De qué color le pintan el pelo a Marisol? – what color do they dye Marisol's hair?

_____

10- ¿Cuánto tiempo pasan en la peluquería? – how long do they stay at the hair salon?

_____

Ejercicio 2

Elige entre "verdadero" o "falso" – choose "true" or "false"

1- **La peluquería se llama Las Cuatro Hermanas.** – The hair salon is called The Four Sisters.

_____

2- **Marisol se corta el cabello con alguien que no conoce.** – Marisol gets a haircut from someone she doesn't know.

_____

3- **La hermana de Marisol se quemó la mano.** – Marisol's sister burned her hand.

_____

4- **El lavado de cabello es relajante.** – The hair wash is relaxing.

_____

5- **Marisol tiene el cabello negro actuamente.** – Marisol currently has black hair.

_____

6- **La hermana de Marisol escoge un color nuevo para ella.** – Marisol's sister chooses a new color for her.

_____

7- **Marisol se corta el cabello ella misma.** – Marisol cuts her own hair.

_____

8- **A Marisol le encanta el nuevo color.** – Marisol loves the new color.

9- **Marisol también se hace las uñas.** – Marisol also gets her nails done.

10- **A la hermana de Marisol no le gusta su corte.** – Marisol's sister doesn't like her own haircut.

Respuestas – Answers

Ejercicio 1

1- Marisol quiere un nuevo look porque está aburrida de su cabello rubio.

2- La cita de Marisol es a las 3 de la tarde.

3- Las revistas son de hace más de quince años.

4- Marisol es descuidada porque se corta todo el tiempo cuando cocina y también se cae en la calle.

5- El champú huele a coco.

6- Marisol quiere que le corten las puntas del cabello y quiere otro color.

7- La hermana de Marisol se corta el cabello ella misma porque a veces tiene las puntas dañadas y no tiene tiempo de ir a la peluquería.

8- La peluquera anterior de Marisol se mudó a Madrid.

9- A Marisol le pintan el cabello de rojo.

10- Marisol y su hermana pasan cuatro horas en la peluquería.

Ejercicio 2

1- Falso

2- Falso

3- Verdadero

4- Verdadero

5- Falso

6- Falso

7- Falso

8- Falso

9- Verdadero

10- Falso

Puntos clave – Key takeaways

- There are only two reciprocal pronouns (*se, nos*).
- Reciprocal pronouns and reflexive pronouns can be often confused since two of them are the same (se, nos). We need to pay attention to the context to see which they are referring to.
- *Querer* has five different conjugations (*quiero, quieres, quiere, queremos, quieren*).
- *Querer* can be followed by another verb (*¿Qué quieres hacer?* = What do you want to do?).
- *Querer* is one of the most common irregular verbs.

In the next chapter, you will learn more about irregular verbs.

Chapter 14:
El escape room – The escape room

El miedo es natural en el prudente,
y el saberlo vencer es ser valiente.
- Alonso de Ercilla y Zúñiga

Tomás y sus amigos van a un escape room el sábado a las 6 de la tarde. Tomás está muy emocionado porque **es su primera vez** en un escape room. Su amigo Luis, **por otra parte**, está nervioso porque es un poco **claustrofóbico, pero igual quiere atreverse** y **vivir la aventura. La chica que recibe a Tomás** y sus cuatro amigos **les cuenta** que hay tres salas diferentes **para escoger**. La primera sala **simula un hospital de noche**, la segunda es **una**

casa embrujada y la tercera sala, **que es la más difícil, simula un avión que está a punto de estrellar. Después**

de pensarlo unos minutos, los chicos deciden probar la tercera sala **porque les gusta el reto. Pagan por sus entradas** y **dejan sus teléfonos, mochilas y carteras** en un locker **afuera de la sala. No saben por qué tienen que hacerlo**, pero **es la única regla que hay.**

Dentro de la sala, la chica **les da las instrucciones.** Les dice que **tienen una hora para salir** de la sala, y **les entrega** un walkie-talkie **para que le pidan pistas si lo necesitan.** También les habla sobre **el botón de emergencia** que **deben presionar en caso de que suceda algo.** La chica cierra la puerta, **el reloj marca una hora y comienza la cuenta regresiva. Apagan las luces.** Todos **comienzan a buscar en todos lados, debajo de los asientos, dentro de las maletas.** Solo tienen **una linterna** así que **el proceso es lento y frustrante.** Una chica encuentra **la primera pista** en **un periódico: números subrayados.** Esto le parece **una especie de combinación.** Tomás **introduce** el número en **un teclado** al lado de una puerta y se abre. Pasan a una pequeña habitación con un enorme **mapa** y **fotos en la pared.** La luz roja **hace que sea más fácil ver.**

Luego, Tomás **se da cuenta de que Luis está bastante pálido.**

–**¿Estás bien?** –pregunta Tomás.

–**Me siento mareado, como que me falta el aire** – responde Luis.

–**¿Quieres irte?**

–No, **acabamos de empezar.**

–**¿Seguro?**

–Sí, **no te preocupes.**

Los chicos **siguen resolviendo los acertijos.** Tomás **organiza los números de los asientos en el orden correcto** y encuentra la contraseña para una pequeña caja fuerte. Dentro de la caja fuerte hay una llave dorada. Tomás la prueba en la única puerta cerrada que queda pero no se abre. Cuando está hablando con la chica en el walkie-talkie, Luis se desmaya.

Todos se alarman. Tocan el botón de emergencia y la chica rápidamente abre la puerta y salen de la habitación llevando a Luis por los hombros. Luis está muy pálido pero reacciona cuando llaman su nombre. Abre los ojos. Parece no recordar lo que pasó. Le dan algo de agua y un chocolate para subirle el nivel de azúcar.

–¿Cómo me desmayé?

–Desmayándote –responde Luis.

–No me acuerdo de nada.

Después de pasar un poco el susto y asegurarse de que Luis está bien, los chicos se van a un café a hablar.

–Nos mataste del susto –dice Tomás.

–Perdón por arruinar la diversión.

–No pasa nada. Lo importante es que estás bien. Igual esa sala era muy fácil, me estaba aburriendo. Tú hiciste las cosas más interesantes.

–No me hagas reír que me duele un poco la cabeza.

–Claro que te duele. Te pegaste en la cabeza con el piso ¿Seguro que no quieres ir al hospital?

–No, estoy bien. La próxima vez vamos a un lugar al aire libre.

Resumen

Tomás y sus amigos deciden pasar un día distinto en un escape room. Tomás en particular está entusiasmado porque es la primera vez que va a uno, mientras que Luis está un poco nervioso por su claustrofobia. Las empleadas los reciben amablemente y les explican todo sobre las salas disponibles y las reglas. Los chicos escogen la tercera sala, una simulación de un avión a punto de estallar. Trabajando en equipo, encuentran diversas pistas y avanzan bastante hasta que Luis se comienza a sentir mal y termina desmayándose. Todos se asustan y lo sacan de la sala, pero al rato Luis se siente mejor y eso es todo lo que importa.

Summary

Tomás and his friend decide to spend a different day at an escape room. Tomás is particularly excited since this is his first time going to one, while Luis is a little nervous because of his claustrophobia. The employees welcome them kindly and explain everything about the rooms available as well as the rules. The guys choose the third room, a simulation of a plane about to explode. Working as a team, they find several clues and get pretty far until Luis starts feeling sick and ends up fainting. They all get scared and take him out of the room, but after a while he feels better and that's all that matters.

Glosario – Glossary

Es su primera vez: it's his first time

Por otra parte: on the other hand

Claustrofóbico: claustrophobic

Pero igual quiere atreverse: but he wants to dare to do it anyway

Vivir la aventura: to live the adventure

La chica que recibe a Tomás: the girl who welcomes Tomás

Les cuenta: tells them

Para escoger: to choose from

Simula un hospital de noche: it simulates a hospital at night

Una casa embrujada: a haunted house

Que es la más difícil: which is the most difficult one

Simula un avión que está a punto de estallar: it simulates a plane that's about to explode

Porque les gusta el reto: because they like a challenge

Pagan por sus entradas: they pay for their tickets

Dejan sus teléfonos, mochilas y carteras: they leave their phones, backpacks and purses

Afuera de la sala: outside of the room

No saben por qué tienen que hacerlo: they don't know why they have to do it

Es la única regla que hay: it's the only rule there is

Dentro de la sala: inside the room

Le da las instrucciones: she gives them instructions

Tienen una hora para salir: they have an hour to get out

Les entrega: she gives them

Para que le pidan pistas si lo necesitan: so they can ask for clues if they need to

El botón de emergencia: the emergency button

Deben presionar en caso de que suceda algo: they must press it if anything goes wrong

El reloj marca una hora: there's one hour on the clock

Comienza la cuenta regresiva: the countdown starts

Apagan las luces: they turn off the lights

Comienzan a buscar en todos lados: they start looking everywhere

Debajo de los asientos: under the seats

Dentro de las maletas: inside the suitcases

Una linterna: a flashlight

El proceso es lento y frustrante: the process is slow and frustrating

La primera pista: the first clue

Un periódico: a newspaper

Números subrayados: highlighted numbers

Una especie de combinación: some kind of combination

Introducir: put

Un teclado: a keyboard

Mapa: map

Fotos en la pared: pictures on the wall

Hace que sea más fácil ver: it makes it easier to see

Se da cuenta de que Luis está pálido: he notices Luis looks pale

¿Estás bien?: are you okay?

Me siento mareado: I feel dizzy

Como que me falta el aire: like I'm out of breath

¿Quieres irte?: do you want to go?

Acabamos de empezar: we just started

¿Seguro?: are you sure?

No te preocupes: don't worry

Siguen resolviendo los acertijos: they keep solving the puzzles

Organiza los números de los asientos en el orden correcto: he puts the seat numbers in the right order

Encuentra la contraseña: he finds the password

Una pequeña caja fuerte: a small safe

Una llave dorada: a golden key

La prueba en la única puerta cerrada que queda: he tries it on the only locked door left

No se abre: it won't open

Cuando está hablando con la chica: when he's talking to the girl

Luis se desmaya: Luis faints

Todos se alarman: they all get alarmed

Tocan el botón de emergencia: they press the emergency button

Rápidamente abre la puerta: she quickly opens the door

Llevando a Luis por los hombros: carrying Luis by the shoulders

Reacciona cuando llaman su nombre: he reacts when they call his name

Abre los ojos: he opens his eyes

No parece recordar lo que pasó: he doesn't seem to remember what happened

Para subirle el nivel de azúcar: to raise his sugar levels

¿Cómo me desmayé?: how did I faint?

Desmayándote: fainting

No me acuerdo: I don't remember anything

Después de pasar el susto: after the scare

Asegurarse de que Luis está bien: making sure Luis is fine

Nos mataste del susto: you scared the life out of us

Perdón por arruinar la diversión: sorry for ruining the fun

No pasa nada: It's okay

Lo importante es que estás bien: What matters is that you're okay.

Igual esa sala era muy fácil: That room was very easy anyway

Me estaba aburriendo: I was getting bored.

Tú hiciste las cosas más interesantes: You made things more interesting.

No me hagas reír: don't make me laugh

Me duele un poco la cabeza: my head hurts a bit

Claro que te duele: of course it hurts

Te pegaste en la cabeza con el piso: you hit your head on the ground

¿Seguro que no quieres ir al hospital?: are you sure you don't want to go to the hospital?

La próxima vez vamos a un lugar al aire libre: next time we'll go someplace outdoors

Ejercicio 1

Contesta las siguientes preguntas – answer the following questions

1- ¿Por qué Luis está nervioso? – why is Luis nervous?

_____

2- ¿Cuántas salas hay para escoger? – how many rooms are there to choose from?

_____

3- ¿Cómo es la segunda sala? – what's the second room like?

_____

4- ¿Cuál es la única regla que hay? – what's the only rule there is?

_____

5- ¿Cuánto tiempo tienen para salir de la sala? – how much time do they have to leave the room?

_____

6- ¿Cuál es la primera pista? – what's the first clue?

_____

7- ¿Qué hay en la nueva habitación? – what's in the new room?

_____

8- ¿Qué hay en la caja fuerte? – what's in the safe?

_____

9- **¿Qué le pasa a Luis?** – what happens to Luis?

_____

10- **¿Por qué a Luis le duele la cabeza?** – why does Luis have a headache?

_____

Ejercicio 2

Elige entre "verdadero" o "falso" – choose "true" or "false"

1- **Esta es la primera vez de Tomás en un escape room.** – This is Tomas's first time in an escape room.

2- **Tomás se aparece con seis amigos.** – Tomás shows up with six friends.

3- **La tercera sala es la más difícil.** – The third room is the hardest.

4- **Tienen solo una linterna.** – They just have one flashlight.

5- **Luis encuentra la primera pista.** – Luis finds the first clue.

6- **La primera pista es un mapa.** – The first clue is a map.

7- **Luis se siente mareado.** – Luis feels dizzy.

8- **Luis decide salir de la sala.** – Luis decides to leave the room.

9- **Los chicos van a un café después.** – They go to a café afterwards.

10- **Los chicos están molestos con Luis por arruinar su diversión.** – They're mad at Luis for ruining their fun.

Respuestas – Answers

Ejercicio 1

1- Luis está nervioso porque es un poco claustrofóbico.

2- Hay tres salas para escoger.

3- La segunda sala es una casa embrujada.

4- La única regla que hay es que deben dejar sus pertenencias en los lockers afuera de la sala.

5- Tienen una hora para salir de la sala.

6- La primera pista es unos números subrayados en un periódico, una especie de combinación.

7- En la nueva habitación hay un enorme mapa y fotos pegadas en la pared.

8- En la caja fuerte hay una llave dorada.

9- Luis se desmaya.

10- A Luis le duele la cabeza porque pegó la cabeza del piso.

Ejercicio 2

1- Verdadero

2- Falso

3- Verdadero

4- Verdadero

5- Falso

6- Falso

7- Verdadero

8- Falso

9- Verdadero

10- Falso

Puntos clave – Key takeaways

- *Hacer* is one of the most common irregular verbs.
- *Hacer* has five different conjugations (*hago, haces, hace, hacemos, hacen*).
- *Hacer* can be followed by another verb (*Me hacer reír* = You make me laugh).
- *Probar* has five different conjugations (*pruebo, pruebas, prueba, probamos, prueban*).
- Irregular verbs can fall into different categories, having small changes when conjugating, or changing completely.

Conclusion

You made it to the end of this book, kudos to you! It wasn't easy, but you put in the work regardless. By reading all the stories and finishing all the exercises compiled in *Learn Spanish with Short Stories for Adult Beginners*, you now have the practice to solidify you as an A1 Spanish learner. All the vocabulary you have learned will aid you in the following steps of your journey. You have learned several ways to greet others and say goodbye, as well as how to express what you do for work, or chat about the hobbies you're passionate about. You can easily talk about numbers, time, days of the week, and colors. You know how to describe someone's appearance in detail or mention traits of their personality. You have the tools to describe the places you visit and talk about the weather there. You can even talk about aspects of your day to day life with ease. You can do all these things now with confidence because you've worked hard for it.

And the best part is, you can always go back to the stories. Any time you're feeling rusty or out of practice, you can review the stories and find comfort while reinforcing what you already know.

Now, we hate to say goodbye, but this doesn't have to end here. By picking up the next book in our series, *Learn Spanish with Short Stories for Adult Beginners 2*, we guarantee more exciting stories that will take your Spanish to the next level. We will be covering more complicated structures from A2, such more irregular verbs in present, as well as the past tenses. The latter, more specifically, tend to be quite challenging for new learners, which is why these stories will be quite valuable in the long run. We hope to see you soon.

$29 FREE BONUSES

Complete Spanish Phrasebook
+ Digital Spanish Flashcards Download

Scan QR code above to claim your free bonuses

OR

visit exploretowin.com/vipbonus

Ready To Start Speaking Spanish?

**Inside this Complete Spanish Phrasebook
+ digital Spanish flashcards combo you'll:**

✓ **Say what you want:** learn the most common words and phrases used in Spanish, so you can express yourself clearly, the first time!

✓ **Avoid awkward fumbling:** explore core Spanish grammar principles to avoid situations where you're left blank, not knowing what to say.

✓ **Improved recall:** Confidently express yourself in Spanish by learning high-frequency verbs & conjugations - taught through fun flashcards!

Scan QR code above to claim your free bonuses

OR

visit exploretowin.com/vipbonus

Made in the USA
Las Vegas, NV
07 March 2024

86831925R00135